SUPER SOUPS

SUPER SOUPS

COLLINS & BROWN

The Good Housekeeping website is
www.goodhousekeeping.co.uk

ISBN 978-1-909397-52-1

A catalogue record for this book is available from
the British Library.

Reproduction by Mission Productions Ltd, Hong
Kong
Printed and bound by 1010 Printing International Ltd,
China

This book can be ordered direct from the publisher.
Contact the marketing department, but try your
bookshop first.

www.anovabooks.com

NOTES

Both metric and imperial measures are given for
the recipes. Follow either set of measures, not a
mixture of both, as they are not interchangeable.

All spoon measures are level.
1 tsp = 5ml spoon; 1 tbsp = 15ml spoon.

Ovens and grills must be preheated to the specified
temperature.

Medium eggs should be used except where
otherwise specified. Free-range eggs are
recommended.

Note that some recipes contain raw or lightly
cooked eggs. The young, elderly, pregnant women
and anyone with an immune-deficiency disease
should avoid these because of the slight risk of
salmonella.

Contents

Everyday Soups

Make Your Own Soup

Soups are nutritious, full of flavour and easy to make. Incredibly versatile, they can be smooth or chunky, light for a first course or substantial for a main course, made with vegetables, pulses, meat, chicken or fish.

You can use almost any mixture of vegetables.

To serve four, you will need:
1 or 2 finely chopped onions, 2 tbsp oil or 1 tbsp oil and 25g (1oz) butter, 1 or 2 crushed garlic cloves (optional), 450g (1lb) chopped mixed vegetables, such as leeks, potatoes, celery, fennel, canned tomatoes and parsnips (finely chopped or cut into larger dice for a chunky soup), 1.1 litres (2 pints) stock.

1 Fry the onions in the oil or oil and butter until soft and add the garlic, if you like.
2 Add the chopped mixed vegetables and the stock. Bring to the boil, then reduce the heat and simmer for 20–30 minutes until the vegetables are tender.
3 Leave chunky, partially purée or blend until smooth.

Puréeing soups

1 **Using a jug blender** Leave the soup to cool slightly, then fill the jug about half-full, making sure that there is more liquid than solids. Cover the lid with a teatowel and hold it on tightly. Blend until smooth, then add more solids and blend again until all the soup is smooth. (If you have a lot of soup, transfer each batch to a clean pan.)

1

2   **Using a stick blender** Leave the soup to cool slightly. Stick the blender deep into the soup, switch it on and move it about so that all the soup is puréed. **Note:** don't do this in a non-stick pan.

3   **Using a mouli-légumes** A mouli-légumes makes a fine purée, although it takes longer than using a blender. Fit the fine plate to the mouli and set it over a bowl – put a teatowel underneath to keep it from moving on the table. Fill the bowl of the mouli about halfway up the sides, putting in more solids than liquid. Work in batches if you have a large quantity of soup.

4   **Using a sieve** If you don't have a blender or mouli-légumes, you can purée the soup by pushing it through a sieve, although this will take a much longer time.

Partially puréed soups

1   For an interesting texture, purée one-third to half of the ingredients, then stir back into the soup.

2   Alternatively, prepare the vegetables or other ingredients, but keep a few choice pieces to one side. While the soup is cooking, steam or boil these pieces until just tender; refresh green vegetables in cold water. Just before serving, cut into smaller pieces and add to the soup.

Chunky soups

1   Cut the ingredients into bite-size pieces. Heat oil or butter in the soup pan and cook the onions – and garlic if you like – until soft and lightly coloured.

2   Add the remaining ingredients, putting in those that need the longest cooking first. Pour in some stock and bring to the boil.

3   Reduce the heat and simmer gently until all the ingredients are tender. If too much liquid boils away, just add more.

Warming Veggie Minestrone

Hands-on time: 15 minutes
Cooking time: 25 minutes

1 onion, roughly chopped

2 celery sticks, roughly chopped

4 small carrots, roughly chopped

1 tbsp vegetable oil

400g can chopped tomatoes

1.4 litres (2½ pints) vegetable stock
   (see page 13)

125g (4oz) spaghetti, broken into
   small pieces

410g can cannellini beans, drained
   and rinsed

150g (5oz) frozen peas

salt and freshly ground black pepper

a small handful of fresh basil to garnish

crusty bread to serve (optional)

1 Pulse the onion, celery and carrots in
   a food processor until chopped to the
   size of peas. Heat the oil in a large
   pan and fry the chopped vegetables
   over a medium heat for 10 minutes
   until soft. Add the tomatoes and
   stock and bring to a simmer.

2 Mix in the spaghetti and simmer for
   10 minutes, adding the beans and
   peas for the final 3 minutes. Check the
   seasoning and ladle into soup bowls.
   Garnish with basil and serve with
   crusty bread, if you like.

Serves 4

Make Your Own Stock

Good stock can make the difference between a good dish and a great one.
It gives depth of flavour to many dishes. There are four main types of stock:
vegetable, meat, chicken and fish. You might not always have time to make
fresh stock so it's a good idea to store a batch in the freezer.

Cook's Tips

❏ To get a clearer liquid when
making fish, meat or poultry stock,
strain the cooked stock through
four layers of muslin in a sieve

❏ Stock will keep for three days in
the fridge. If you want to keep it
for a further three days, transfer
it to a pan and reboil gently for 5
minutes. Cool, put in a clean bowl
and chill for a further three days

❏ When making meat or chicken
stock, make sure there is a good
ratio of meat to bones. The more
meat you use, the more flavour the
stock will have

Vegetable Stock

For 1.1 litres (2 pints), you will need:
225g (8oz) each chopped onion,
celery, leek and carrot, 2 bay leaves,
a few fresh thyme sprigs, 1 small
bunch of fresh parsley, 10 black
peppercorns, ½ tsp salt.

1   Put all the ingredients into a
    pan and pour in 1.7 litres (3 pints)
    cold water.
2   Bring slowly to the boil and
    skim the surface. Reduce the
    heat, partially cover the pan and
    simmer gently for 30 minutes.
    Adjust the seasoning if necessary.
3   Strain the stock through a fine
    sieve into a bowl and leave to cool.

Meat Stock

For 900ml (1½ pints), you will need:
450g (1lb) each meat bones and
stewing meat, 1 onion, 2 celery sticks
and 1 large carrot, sliced, 1 bouquet
garni (2 bay leaves, a few thyme
sprigs, 1 small bunch of parsley),
1 tsp black peppercorns, ½ tsp salt.

1   Preheat the oven to 220°C (200°C
    fan oven) mark 7. Put the meat
    and bones into a roasting tin and
    roast for 30–40 minutes, turning
    now and again, until they are
    well browned.
2   Put the bones into a large pan
    with the remaining ingredients
    and add 2 litres (3½ pints) cold
    water. Bring slowly to the boil
    and skim the surface.
3   Partially cover the pan and
    simmer for 4–5 hours. Adjust the
    seasoning if necessary. Strain
    through a muslin-lined sieve into
    a bowl and cool quickly. Degrease
    (see page 15) before using.

Fish Stock

For 900ml (1½ pints), you will need:
900g (2lb) washed fish bones
and trimmings, 2 chopped carrots,
1 chopped onion and 2 sliced celery
sticks, 1 bouquet garni (2 bay leaves,
a few fresh thyme sprigs and a small
bunch of fresh parsley), 6 white
peppercorns, ½ tsp salt.

1 Put all the ingredients into a
   large pan with 900ml (1½ pints)
   cold water.
2 Bring slowly to the boil and
   skim the surface. Reduce the
   heat, partially cover the pan and
   simmer gently for 30 minutes.
   Adjust the seasoning if necessary.
3 Strain the stock through a muslin-
   lined sieve into a bowl and cool
   quickly. Fish stock tends not to
   have much fat in it and so does
   not usually need to be degreased.
   However, if it does seem to be
   fatty, you will need to remove this
   by degreasing it (see opposite).

Chicken Stock

For 1.1 litres (2 pints), you will need:
1.6kg (3½lb) chicken bones or a
stripped roast chicken carcass,
225g (8oz) each sliced onions and
celery, 150g (5oz) chopped leeks,
1 bouquet garni (2 bay leaves, a
few fresh thyme sprigs and a small
bunch of fresh parsley), 1 tsp black
peppercorns, ½ tsp salt.

1 Put all the ingredients into a
   large pan with 3 litres (5¼ pints)
   cold water.
2 Bring slowly to the boil and
   skim the surface. Reduce the
   heat, partially cover the pan and
   simmer gently for 2 hours. Adjust
   the seasoning if necessary.
3 Strain the stock through a muslin-
   lined sieve into a bowl and cool
   quickly. Degrease (see opposite)
   before using.

Degreasing stock

Meat and poultry stock needs to be degreased. (Vegetable stock does not.) You can mop the fat from the surface using kitchen paper, but the following methods are easier and more effective. There are three main methods that you can use: ladling, pouring and chilling.

1 **Ladling** While the stock is warm, place a ladle on the surface. Press down to allow the fat floating on the surface to trickle over the edge until the ladle is full. Discard the fat, then repeat until all the fat has been removed.

2 **Pouring** For this you need a degreasing jug or a double-pouring gravy boat, which has the spout at the bottom of the vessel. When you fill the jug or gravy boat with a fatty liquid, the fat rises. When you pour, the stock comes out while the fat stays behind in the jug.

3 **Chilling** This technique works best with stock made from meat, whose fat solidifies when cold. Put the stock in the fridge until the fat becomes solid, then remove the pieces of fat using a slotted spoon.

Carrot and Coriander Soup

Hands-on time: 15 minutes
Cooking time: about 30 minutes

40g (1½oz) butter

175g (6oz) leeks, trimmed and sliced

450g (1lb) carrots, sliced

2 tsp ground coriander

1 tsp plain flour

1.2 litres (2 pints) hot vegetable stock
   (see page 13)

150ml (¼ pint) single cream

salt and freshly ground black pepper

fresh coriander leaves, roughly torn,
   to serve

1 Melt the butter in a large pan. Stir in the leeks and carrots, then cover the pan and cook gently for 7–10 minutes until the vegetables begin to soften but not colour.

2 Stir in the ground coriander and flour and cook, stirring, for 1 minute.

3 Add the hot stock and bring to the boil, stirring. Season with salt and ground black pepper, then reduce the heat, cover the pan and simmer for about 20 minutes until the vegetables are tender.

4 Leave the soup to cool a little, then whiz in batches in a blender or food processor until smooth. Return to the pan and stir in the cream. Adjust the seasoning and reheat gently – do not boil.

5 Ladle into warmed bowls, scatter with torn coriander leaves and serve.

Serves 6

Leek and Potato Soup

Hands-on time: 10 minutes
Cooking time: 45 minutes

25g (1oz) butter

1 onion, finely chopped

1 garlic clove, crushed

550g (1¼lb) leeks, trimmed and chopped

200g (7oz) floury potatoes, peeled and sliced

1.3 litres (2¼ pints) hot vegetable stock (see page 13)

crème fraîche and chopped chives to garnish

1 Melt the butter in a pan over a gentle heat. Add the onion and cook for 10–15 minutes until soft. Add the garlic and cook for a further 1 minute. Add the leeks and cook for 5–10 minutes until softened. Add the potatoes and toss together with the leeks.

2 Pour in the hot stock and bring to the boil, then reduce the heat and simmer the soup for 20 minutes until the potatoes are tender.

3 Leave the soup to cool a little, then whiz in batches in a blender or food processor until smooth.

4 Reheat the soup gently. Ladle into warmed bowls, garnish with crème fraîche and chives and serve.

Serves 4

Mixed Mushroom Soup

Hands-on time: 15 minutes, plus soaking
Cooking time: 35 minutes

5g (⅓oz) dried porcini mushrooms

1 tbsp sunflower oil, plus 50ml (2fl oz) to shallow-fry

1 small onion, chopped

450g (1lb) chestnut mushrooms, chopped

600ml (1 pint) hot vegetable stock (see page 13)

2 slices white bread, crusts removed, cut into cubes

2 garlic cloves, finely sliced

salt and freshly ground black pepper

freshly chopped flat-leafed parsley to garnish

a drizzle of cream to serve

1 Put the porcini into a bowl, pour over 75ml (2½fl oz) boiling water and leave to soak for 10 minutes. Strain the porcini, put the liquid to one side, then chop roughly, keeping 1 tbsp to use as a garnish.

2 Heat the 1 tbsp oil in a pan. Add the onion and porcini, and cook over a medium heat for 5 minutes. Add the chestnut mushrooms, increase the heat and brown lightly for 5 minutes. Add the reserved porcini liquid and the hot stock, then bring to the boil. Season well with salt and ground black pepper, then reduce the heat and simmer for 20 minutes.

3 To make croûtons, heat 50ml (2fl oz) oil in a frying pan. Add the bread and garlic, and stir-fry for 2 minutes until golden. Drain on kitchen paper.

4 Take the soup off the heat and leave to cool slightly. Purée in a food processor or blender until smooth, then transfer to a clean pan. Reheat gently, then divide among four warmed bowls. Top with the croûtons, reserved porcini and a sprinkling of parsley, then drizzle with cream and serve.

Serves 4

Broccoli and Goat's Cheese Soup

Hands-on time: 10 minutes
Cooking time: 30 minutes

50g (2oz) butter

2 medium onions, chopped

1 litre (1¾ pints) vegetable, chicken or
  turkey stock (see pages 13 and 14)

700g (1½lb) broccoli, broken into florets,
  stout stalks peeled and chopped

1 head of garlic, separated into cloves

1 tbsp olive oil

150g (5oz) goat's cheese

salt and freshly ground black pepper

1 Preheat the oven to 200°C (180°C
  fan oven) mark 6. Melt the butter in a
  saucepan over a gentle heat. Add the
  onions, then cover the pan and cook
  for 4–5 minutes until translucent. Add
  half the stock and bring to the boil.
  Add the broccoli and bring back to the
  boil, then cover the pan, reduce the
  heat and simmer for 15–20 minutes
  or until the broccoli is tender.

2 Meanwhile, toss the cloves of garlic
  in the oil and tip into a roasting tin.
  Roast in the oven for 15 minutes until
  soft when squeezed.

3 Leave the soup to cool a little, then
  add the goat's cheese and whiz in
  batches in a blender or food processor
  until smooth. Pour the soup back into
  the pan and add the remaining stock.
  Reheat gently on the hob and season
  to taste with salt and pepper.

4 Ladle the soup into warmed bowls,
  squeeze the garlic out of their skins
  and scatter over the soup, add a
  sprinkling of black pepper and serve.

Serves 6

Cream of Chicken Soup

Hands-on time: 10 minutes
Cooking time: 30 minutes

3 tbsp plain flour

150ml (¼ pint) milk

1.1 litres (2 pints) chicken stock
(see page 14)

125g (4oz) cooked chicken, diced

1 tsp lemon juice

a pinch of freshly grated nutmeg

2 tbsp single cream

salt and freshly ground black pepper

croûtons and parsley sprigs to garnish

1 Put the flour into a large bowl, add a little of the milk and blend until it makes a smooth cream.

2 Bring the stock to the boil, then stir it into the blended mixture. Pour back into the pan and simmer gently for 20 minutes.

3 Stir in the chicken, lemon juice and nutmeg and season to taste with salt and ground black pepper. Mix the rest of the milk with the cream and stir in, then reheat without boiling.

4 Taste and adjust the seasoning. Ladle the soup into warmed bowls, sprinkle with croûtons and parsley sprigs and serve.

Serves 4

Chicken Noodle Soup

Hands-on time: 15 minutes
Cooking time: 20 minutes

2 medium eggs

1.6 litres (2¾ pints) chicken stock
(see page 14)

1 tbsp light soy sauce

2cm (¾in) piece fresh root ginger,
peeled and thickly sliced

1 garlic clove, bruised

3 skinless chicken breasts

2 carrots, finely chopped

125g (4oz) fine or medium noodles

150g (5oz) oyster mushrooms

salt and freshly ground black pepper

4 spring onions, finely sliced, to garnish

1 Bring a small pan of water to the boil; simmer the eggs for 7 minutes. Drain, put in a bowl and cover with cold water.

2 Meanwhile, heat the stock, soy sauce, ginger and garlic in a large pan and bring to the boil. Add the chicken, reduce the heat and simmer for 12 minutes until the meat is cooked through. Lift the meat out of the broth and on to a board. Discard the ginger and garlic. Add the carrots and noodles to the broth. Simmer for 4 minutes and season to taste. Meanwhile, slice the chicken breast and shell and halve the eggs.

3 Divide the soup among four bowls (adding a little more boiling water if needed), top each with a quarter of the chicken slices, a quarter of the mushrooms and half an egg. Scatter over the spring onions and serve.

Serves 4

Scotch Broth

🍴 **Hands-on time:** 15 minutes
Cooking time: about 1 hour

1 tbsp vegetable oil

250g (9oz) lamb neck fillets, cut into
   2cm (¾in) cubes

2 parsnips, roughly chopped

2 carrots, roughly chopped

1 onion, finely chopped

1 potato, finely diced

3 smoked streaky bacon rashers,
   finely sliced

125g (4oz) pearl barley

1 litre (1¾ pints) lamb stock

75g (3oz) frozen peas

salt and freshly ground black pepper

a small handful of finely chopped
   fresh parsley to garnish

1 Heat the oil over a high heat in a large casserole. Brown the lamb all over – do this in batches if necessary to stop the lamb from sweating rather than browning. Add the parsnips, carrots, onion, potato and bacon and fry for 3–5 minutes.

2 Add the pearl barley and mix well. Pour in the stock and stir well, scraping any sticky goodness from the bottom of the casserole. Bring to the boil, then reduce the heat, cover and simmer gently for 40–50 minutes until the lamb is tender.

3 Stir in the peas, heat through, then check the seasoning. Transfer to individual bowls, garnish the broth with parsley and serve.

SAVE MONEY

Neck is an ideal cut of lamb to use
if you are watching your wallet.

Pea and Ham Soup

Hands-on time: 10 minutes
Cooking time: about 15 minutes

1 tbsp oil

1 onion, chopped

750g (1lb 11oz) frozen peas

1 litre (1¾ pints) chicken stock
(see page 14)

2 x 200g (7oz) unsmoked gammon
steaks, trimmed of fat

1 tbsp freshly chopped chives, plus extra
to garnish

4 tsp half-fat crème fraîche

crusty bread to serve

1 Heat the oil in a large pan and fry the onion for 10 minutes until softened but not coloured.

2 Stir in the peas and chicken stock and bring to the boil. Add the gammon steaks and simmer for 5 minutes until cooked through.

3 Lift out the gammon and set aside on a board. Blend the soup until completely smooth (do this in batches, if necessary). Meanwhile, shred the gammon into fine pieces, discarding any fat.

4 Return the soup to the pan, reheat, and add the shredded gammon and chives. Check the seasoning. Divide among four warmed soup bowls and garnish with some crème fraîche, extra chives and ground black pepper. Serve with crusty bread.

Serves 4

Perfect Prawns

Full of flavour, raw prawns are delicious used in soup.
They can be cooked in or out of their shells.

Peeling and butterflying

1 To peel prawns, pull off the head
   and put to one side. Using pointed
   scissors, cut through the soft shell
   on the belly side.

2 Prise the shell off, leaving
   the tail attached. (Add to the head;
   it can be used later for making
   stock.)

3 Using a small sharp knife, make a
   shallow cut along the length of the
   back of the prawn. Use the point of
   the knife to carefully remove and
   discard the black vein (intestinal
   tract) that runs along the back of
   the prawn.

4 To 'butterfly' the prawn, cut halfway through the flesh lengthways from the head end to the base of the tail, and open up the prawn.

4

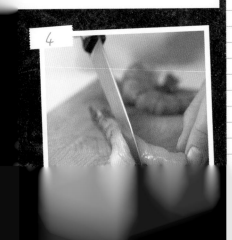

Langoustines and crayfish

Related to the prawn, langoustines and crayfish can be peeled in the same way as prawns. To extract the meat from langoustine claws, pull off the small pincer from the claws, then work with small scissors to cut open the main section all the way along its length. Split open and carefully pull out the flesh in a single piece. To extract the meat from large crayfish claws, crack them open using a hammer or lobster cracker, then carefully remove the meat.

Also known as scampi, langoustines can be used in a shellfish soup.

Crayfish are sold either live or cooked. To cook, boil in court bouillon for 5–10 minutes. Remove from the stock and cool. Eat crayfish from the shell or in a soup.

Fast Fish Soup

Hands-on time: 10 minutes
Cooking time: about 15 minutes

1 leek, trimmed and finely chopped
4 fat garlic cloves, crushed
3 celery sticks, finely chopped
1 small fennel bulb, finely chopped
1 red chilli, seeded and finely chopped
   (see page 78)
3 tbsp olive oil
50ml (2fl oz) dry white wine
about 750g (1lb 11oz) mixed fish and
   shellfish, such as haddock and
   monkfish fillets, peeled and deveined
   raw prawns (see page 32), and fresh
   mussels, scrubbed and cleaned
   (discard any mussels that don't close
   when tapped on a worksurface or that
   have broken shells, see page 132)
4 tomatoes, chopped
20g (¼oz) freshly chopped thyme
salt and freshly ground black pepper

1 Put the leek into a large pan and add the garlic, celery, fennel, chilli and oil. Cook over a medium heat for 5 minutes or until the vegetables are soft and beginning to colour.

2 Stir in 1.1 litres (2 pints) boiling water and the wine. Bring to the boil, then reduce the heat, cover the pan and simmer for 5 minutes.

3 Cut the white fish into large chunks. Add to the soup with the tomatoes and thyme. Continue to simmer gently until the fish has just turned opaque. Add the prawns, simmer for 1 minute, then add the mussels, if you're using them.

4 As soon as all the mussels have opened (discard any that do not), season the soup with salt and ground black pepper. Ladle into warmed bowls and serve immediately.

Serves 4

Make It Go Further

Before doing your weekly shop, have a good look at the ingredients in your fridge and vegetable rack and think of ways to use them up. You can then go out and buy the ingredients you need to make the most of the items you already have.

Clever leftovers

We all struggle with portion sizing and often have extra rice, potatoes or other ingredients left at the end of each meal. There is a difference between leftovers and waste food. Leftovers are the bits and pieces that sit in a clingfilm-covered bowl in your fridge, challenging you to use them creatively. If you ignore them for four or five days they become waste. Why not try making the most of your leftover bits and bobs?

Ways of using leftovers

There are many ways of using leftover food and slightly over-ripe fruit and vegetables that are starting to wilt. You can:

- ❑ Simply add the ingredients to a stir-fry, pasta bake, soup, risotto... the list is endless
- ❑ 'Stretch' the ingredients – sometimes the amount left over is so small it won't go very far in a family setting. Try adding to it. You can cook a little more of it (for example, rice), or try adding lentils and tomatoes to leftover mince to create a whole new take on Bolognese sauce
- ❑ Make the most of fruit and vegetables that are starting to wilt

Alternative suggestions

You may not always feel like transforming your leftovers into meals – or there may not be enough to do so. Another option is to freeze the odd ingredient for later use.

Small amounts of herbs – freeze in ice cube trays

One or two chillies – these freeze well and are easy to chop from frozen

Double cream – lightly whip the cream and then freeze

Cheese – hard cheeses will become crumbly once thawed, but can be used for grating or in cooking

Bread – whiz in a food processor to make breadcrumbs: these freeze well in a sealed plastic bag

Leftover Roast Chicken Soup

3 tbsp olive oil, 1 chopped onion, 1 chopped carrot, 2 chopped celery sticks, 2 chopped fresh thyme sprigs, 1 bay leaf, a stripped roast chicken carcass, 150–200g (5–7oz) chopped roast chicken, 200g (7oz) mashed or roast potato, 1 tbsp double cream, salt and freshly ground black pepper.

1 Heat the oil in a large pan. Add the onion, carrot, celery and thyme and fry gently for 20–30 minutes until soft but not brown. Add the bay leaf, chicken carcass and 900ml (1½ pints) boiling water to the pan. Bring to the boil, then reduce the heat and simmer for 5 minutes.

2 Remove the bay leaf and carcass and add the chopped roast chicken and cooked potato to the pan. Simmer for 5 minutes.

3 Whiz the soup in a food processor, pour back into the pan and bring to the boil. Stir in the cream, check the seasoning and serve immediately.

Meat-free Soups

Chilled Asparagus Soup

Hands-on time: 5 minutes, plus chilling
Cooking time: 25 minutes

1.1kg (2½lb) asparagus, trimmed
3 tbsp olive oil
4 large shallots, finely chopped
200g (7oz) leeks, trimmed and
   finely chopped
salt and freshly ground black pepper
chervil sprigs and crusty bread to serve

1 Cut the tips off the asparagus and put to one side. Cut the stalks into 2.5cm (1in) lengths.
2 Heat the oil in a large pan, add the shallots and cook gently for 2–3 minutes. Add the leeks and cook, stirring occasionally, for about 10 minutes or until they are soft.
3 Add the asparagus stalks and 900ml (1½ pints) water and season to taste with salt and pepper. Bring to the boil, reduce the heat and simmer very gently, uncovered, for 10 minutes or until the asparagus is soft.
4 Leave the soup to cool a little, then whiz in a blender or food processor until smooth. Pour into a bowl and leave to cool.
5 Add the asparagus tips to a pan of lightly salted boiling water and cook for 2–3 minutes until tender. Drain and refresh under cold running water.
6 Add the asparagus tips to the soup, cover and chill for several hours.
7 To serve, stir about 450ml (¾ pint) iced water into the soup to obtain the required consistency. Season generously with salt and ground black pepper. Ladle into chilled bowls, top with chervil and serve with crusty bread.

Serves 6

Gazpacho with Tortilla Chips

Hands-on time: 30 minutes, plus chilling

900g (2lb) ripe tomatoes

4 garlic cloves

50g (2oz) fresh white breadcrumbs

6 tbsp extra virgin olive oil

juice of 1½ small limes

1 red chilli, seeded and chopped
  (see page 78)

2 cucumbers, seeded and chopped

2 bunches of spring onions, chopped

1 red pepper, seeded and chopped

600ml (1 pint) tomato juice

6 tbsp freshly chopped coriander

salt and freshly ground black pepper

175g bag tortilla chips to serve

To garnish

1 large avocado

juice of ½ small lime

140ml (4½fl oz) soured cream

a few fresh coriander sprigs, chopped

1 Score a cross in the skin at the base of each tomato, then put into a bowl. Pour over enough boiling water to cover them, leave for 30 seconds, then transfer to a bowl of cold water. Peel, discarding the skins, then cut into quarters. Discard the seeds.

2 Put all the gazpacho ingredients into a large bowl and mix well, then whiz together in batches in a blender or food processor until smooth. Transfer to a bowl or jug, season generously with salt and ground black pepper and stir the soup well. Cover and chill for at least 2 hours or overnight.

3 Just before serving, peel and roughly dice the avocado, then toss in lime juice to coat. Ladle the soup into chilled bowls, garnish with soured cream, the avocado, a sprinkling of black pepper and chopped coriander and serve the tortilla chips separately.

Serves 8

Iced Sweet Pepper Soup

Hands-on time: 5 minutes, plus chilling
Cooking time: 20 minutes

4 tbsp freshly chopped coriander

2 medium red peppers, seeded and sliced

1 medium onion, sliced

225g (8oz) ripe tomatoes, sliced

900ml (1½ pints) vegetable stock (see page 13)

150ml (¼ pint) milk

salt and freshly ground black pepper

1 First make coriander ice cubes. Put the chopped coriander into an ice-cube tray, top up with water and freeze.

2 Put the peppers into a large saucepan with the onion, tomatoes and stock. Bring to the boil, then reduce the heat, cover the pan and simmer for about 15 minutes or until the vegetables are tender. Drain, putting the liquid to one side.

3 Whiz the vegetables in a blender or food processor until smooth, then sieve the purée to remove the tomato seeds.

4 Combine the reserved liquid, vegetable purée and milk in a bowl with salt and ground black pepper to taste. Cool for 30 minutes, then chill for at least 2 hours before serving. Ladle into chilled bowls and serve with coriander ice cubes.

Serves 4

Perfect Tomatoes

Tomatoes add a rich flavour to many soups.
Follow the steps below for perfect tomato preparation.

Seeding tomatoes

1. Halve the tomato through the core. Using a spoon or a small sharp knife, remove the seeds and juice, then shake off the excess liquid.
2. Chop the tomato as required for your recipe and place in a colander for a minute or two, to drain off any excess liquid.

Cutting Tomatoes

1. Use a small sharp knife to cut out the core in a single cone-shaped piece. Discard the core.

Wedges Halve the tomato and then cut into quarters or into three.

Slices Hold the tomato with the cored side on the chopping board for greater stability and use a serrated knife to cut into slices.

1

Peeling tomatoes

1   Fill a bowl or pan with boiling
    water. Using a slotted spoon,
    carefully add the tomato and leave
    for 15–30 seconds, then put on a
    chopping board.
2   Using a small sharp knife, cut out
    the core in a single cone-shaped
    piece. Discard the core.
3   Peel off the skin; it should come
    away easily, depending on
    ripeness.

Sweet Potato Soup

Hands-on time: 20 minutes
Cooking time: 35 minutes

1 tbsp olive oil

1 large onion, finely chopped

2 tsp coriander seeds, crushed

2 fresh red chillies, seeded and chopped
(see page 78)

1 butternut squash, about 750g (1lb 10oz),
peeled and roughly chopped

2 sweet potatoes, peeled and
roughly chopped

2 tomatoes, peeled and diced

1.7 litres (3 pints) hot vegetable stock
(see page 13)

freshly ground black pepper and
cheese straws to serve

1 Heat the oil in a large pan over a gentle heat. Add the onion and fry for about 10 minutes until soft. Add the coriander seeds and chillies to the pan and cook for 1-2 minutes.

2 Add the squash, sweet potatoes and tomatoes and cook for 5 minutes. Add the hot stock, cover and bring to the boil, then reduce the heat and simmer gently for 15 minutes or until the vegetables are soft.

3 Leave the soup to cool a little, then whiz in batches in a blender or food processor until smooth. Reheat gently and serve with a sprinkling of black pepper and cheese straws.

FREEZE AHEAD

To make ahead and freeze, complete the recipe, then cool, pack and freeze for up to three months. To use, thaw for 4 hours at cool room temperature. Put in a pan, bring to the boil, reduce the heat and simmer for 10 minutes.

Serves 8

Autumn Barley Soup

Hands-on time: 10 minutes
Cooking time: 1 hour 5 minutes

25g (1oz) pot barley, washed and drained

1 litre (1¾ pints) vegetable stock
  (see page 13)

2 large carrots, diced

1 turnip, peeled and diced

2 leeks, trimmed and sliced

2 celery sticks, diced

1 small onion, finely chopped

1 bouquet garni

2 tbsp freshly chopped parsley

salt and freshly ground black pepper

1 Put the barley and stock into a pan and bring to the boil. Reduce the heat and simmer for 45 minutes until tender.

2 Add the vegetables to the pan with the bouquet garni and season to taste with ground black pepper. Bring to the boil, then reduce the heat and simmer for about 20 minutes or until the vegetables are tender.

3 Discard the bouquet garni. Add the parsley to the soup, season to taste with salt and ground black pepper and stir well, then ladle into warmed bowls and serve immediately.

Serves 4

Beetroot Soup

🍴 **Hands-on time:** 15 minutes
Cooking time: about 45 minutes

1 tbsp olive oil

1 onion, finely chopped

750g (1lb 11oz) raw beetroot, peeled and
cut into 1cm (½in) cubes

275g (10oz) potatoes, roughly chopped

2 litres (3½ pints) hot vegetable stock
(see page 13)

juice of 1 lemon

salt and freshly ground black pepper

To serve

125ml (4fl oz) soured cream

25g (1oz) mixed root vegetable crisps
(optional)

2 tbsp snipped fresh chives

1 Heat the oil in a large pan. Add the
onion and cook for 5 minutes to
soften. Add the beetroot and potatoes
and cook for a further 5 minutes.

2 Add the hot stock and the lemon
juice and bring to the boil. Season
with salt and ground black pepper,
then reduce the heat and simmer,
half-covered, for 25 minutes. Leave
the soup to cool a little, then whiz in
batches in a blender or food processor
until smooth.

3 Pour into a clean pan and reheat
gently. Ladle into warmed bowls. Swirl
1 tbsp soured cream on each portion,
scatter with a few vegetable crisps, if
you like, and sprinkle with snipped
chives to serve.

FREEZE AHEAD

To make ahead and freeze, prepare the soup to the end of step 2. Next, cool half or all the soup, pack and freeze for up to three months. To use, thaw the soup overnight and simmer over a low heat for 5 minutes.

Serves 8

Easy Pea Soup

Hands-on time: 2 minutes, plus thawing
Cooking time: 15 minutes

1 small baguette, thinly sliced

2 tbsp basil-infused olive oil, plus extra to drizzle

450g (1lb) frozen peas, thawed

600ml (1 pint) vegetable stock (see page 13)

salt and freshly ground black pepper

1 Preheat the oven to 220°C (200°C fan oven) mark 7. To make the croûtons, put the bread on a baking sheet, drizzle with 2 tbsp oil and bake for 10–15 minutes until golden.

2 Meanwhile, put the peas in a food processor, add the stock and season with salt and ground black pepper. Whiz for 2–3 minutes.

3 Pour the soup into a pan and bring to the boil, then reduce the heat and simmer for 10 minutes. Spoon into warmed bowls, add the croûtons, drizzle with extra oil and sprinkle with salt and pepper. Serve immediately.

Serves 4

Lettuce Soup

Hands-on time: 5 minutes
Cooking time: 1–1¼ hours

50g (2oz) butter

350g (12oz) lettuce leaves,
roughly chopped

125g (4oz) spring onions, trimmed and
roughly chopped

1 tbsp plain wholemeal flour

600ml (1 pint) vegetable stock
(see page 13)

150ml (¼ pint) milk

salt and freshly ground black pepper

soured cream to serve (optional)

1 Melt the butter in a deep pan, add the
   lettuce and spring onions and cook
   gently for about 10 minutes until
   very soft.

2 Stir in the flour and cook, stirring, for
   1 minute, then add the stock. Bring to
   the boil, then reduce the heat, cover
   the pan and simmer for 45 minutes
   to 1 hour.

3 Leave the soup to cool a little, then
   whiz in batches in a blender or food
   processor until smooth. Pour back into
   the rinsed-out pan and add the milk
   with salt and ground black pepper to
   taste. Reheat to serving temperature.

4 Ladle into warmed bowls and
   finish with a swirl of soured cream,
   if you like.

Serves 4

Spinach and Rice Soup

Hands-on time: 10 minutes
Cooking time: 30 minutes

4 tbsp extra virgin olive oil,
   plus extra to serve

1 onion, finely chopped

2 garlic cloves, crushed

2 tsp freshly chopped thyme or
   a large pinch of dried thyme

2 tsp freshly chopped rosemary or
   a large pinch of dried rosemary

zest of ½ lemon

2 tsp ground coriander

¼ tsp cayenne pepper

125g (4oz) arborio rice

1.1 litres (2 pints) vegetable stock
   (see page 13)

225g (8oz) spinach, fresh or frozen and
   thawed, shredded

4 tbsp pesto, fresh ready-made

salt and freshly ground black pepper

Parmesan, freshly grated, to serve

1 Heat half the oil in a pan. Add the onion, garlic, herbs, lemon zest and spices, then fry gently for 5 minutes.

2 Add the remaining oil with the rice and cook, stirring, for 1 minute. Add the stock and bring to the boil, then reduce the heat and simmer gently for 20 minutes or until the rice is tender.

3 Stir the spinach into the soup with the pesto. Cook for 2 minutes, then season to taste with salt and ground black pepper.

4 Ladle into warmed bowls and serve drizzled with a little oil and topped with Parmesan.

Serves 4

Cream of Parsley Soup

Hands-on time: 15 minutes, plus chilling
Cooking time: 45 minutes

50g (2oz) butter or polyunsaturated
  margarine

225g (8oz) parsley, roughly chopped

2 medium onions, sliced

125g (4oz) celery, sliced

3 tbsp plain wholemeal flour

2 litres (3½ pints) vegetable stock
  (see page 13)

150ml (¼ pint) single cream

salt and freshly ground black pepper

fresh parsley sprigs to garnish

1 Melt the butter or margarine in a large pan. Add the parsley, onions and celery, cover the pan and cook gently for about 10 minutes until the vegetables are soft. Shake the pan occasionally.

2 Stir in the flour until smooth, then mix in the stock. Season with salt and ground black pepper to taste and bring to the boil, then reduce the heat, cover and simmer for 25–30 minutes.

3 Leave the soup to cool a little, then whiz in batches in a blender or food processor until smooth. Leave to cool completely, then chill.

4 Reheat the soup until bubbling, then taste and adjust the seasoning and swirl in the cream. Ladle into eight warmed bowls, garnish with parsley sprigs and serve.

Serves 8

Spicy Soups

Spices and Sauces

Most spices are sold dried, either whole or ground. For optimum flavour, buy whole spices and grind them yourself.

Spices

Cayenne pepper is made from small, hot dried red chillies. It is always sold ground and is sweet, pungent and very hot. Use it sparingly. Unlike paprika, cayenne pepper cannot be used for colouring as its flavour is too pronounced.

Chilli, available as powder or flakes as well as fresh, is a fiery hot spice and should be used cautiously. Some brands, often called mild chilli powder or chilli seasoning, are a mixture of chilli and other flavourings, such as cumin, oregano, salt and garlic; these are therefore considerably less fiery than hot chilli powder. Adjust the quantity you use accordingly.

Cinnamon is the dried, rolled bark of a tropical evergreen tree. Available as sticks and in powdered form, it has a sweet, pungent flavour. Cinnamon sticks have a more pronounced flavour than the powder, but they are difficult to grind at home, so buy ready-ground cinnamon for use in sweet, spicy baking. Use cinnamon sticks to flavour meat casseroles, vegetable dishes, chutneys and pickles.

Coriander seeds have a mild, sweet, orangey flavour and taste quite different from the fresh green leaves, which are used as a herb. Sold whole or ground, they are an ingredient of most curry powders.

Cumin has a strong, slightly bitter taste, improved by toasting. Sold whole as seeds, or ground, it is an ingredient of curry powders and some chilli powder mixtures.

Curry leaves have a fresh-tasting flavour akin to curry powder. They are used as a herb in cooking, most often added whole, but sometimes chopped first. The fresh or dried leaves can be used sparingly to flavour soups and stews. Sold fresh in bunches, curry leaves can be frozen in a plastic bag and added to dishes as required.

Fenugreek seeds are yellow-brown and very hard, with a distinctive aroma and slightly harsh, hot flavour. An ingredient of commercial curry powders, fenugreek is also used in chutneys, pickles and sauces.

Nutmeg, seed of the nutmeg fruit, has a distinctive, nutty flavour. Sold whole or ground, but best bought whole since the flavour of freshly grated nutmeg is far superior.

Paprika is a sweet mild spice made from certain varieties of red pepper; it is always sold ground to a red powder. It is good for adding colour to pale egg and cheese dishes. Some varieties, particularly Hungarian, are hotter than others. Paprika doesn't keep its flavour well, so buy little and often. Produced from oak-smoked red peppers, smoked paprika has an intense flavour and wonderful smoky aroma. Sweet, bittersweet and hot-smoked varieties are available.

Saffron, the most expensive of all spices, is the dried stigma of the saffron crocus flower. It has a wonderful subtle flavour and aroma and imparts a hint of yellow to foods it is cooked with. Powdered saffron is available, but it is the whole stigmas, called saffron strands or threads, that give the best results. A generous pinch is all that is needed to flavour and colour dishes.

Turmeric is a member of the ginger family, though it is rarely available fresh. The bright orange root is commonly dried, then ground and sold in powdered form. Turmeric powder has an aromatic, slightly bitter flavour and should be used sparingly in curry powder, pickles, relishes and rice dishes. Like saffron, turmeric colours the foods it is cooked with, but it has a much harsher flavour than saffron.

Thai green curry paste is a blend of spices such as green chillies, coriander and lemongrass. Thai red curry paste contains fresh and dried red chillies and ginger. Once opened, store in a sealed container in the fridge.

Sauces

Soy sauce – made from fermented soya beans and, usually, wheat, this is the most common flavouring in Chinese and South-east Asian cooking. There are light and dark soy sauces; the dark kind is slightly sweeter and tends to darken the food. It will keep indefinitely.

Tabasco – a fiery hot sauce based on red chillies, spirit vinegar and salt, and prepared to a secret recipe. A dash of Tabasco may be used to add a kick to soups, casseroles, sauces, rice dishes and tomato-based drinks.

Thai fish sauce – a salty condiment with a distinctive, pungent aroma. It is used in many South-east Asian dishes. You can buy it in most large supermarkets and Asian food stores. It will keep indefinitely.

Coconut milk

Canned coconut milk is widely available, but if you can't find it, use blocks of creamed coconut or coconut powder, following the packet instructions to make the amount of liquid you need.

Which oil to use?

Groundnut (peanut) oil has a mild flavour and is well suited to stir-frying and deep-frying as it has a high smoke point and can therefore be used at high temperatures.

Sesame oil has a distinctive nutty flavour; it is best used in marinades or added as a seasoning to stir-fried dishes just before serving.

Vegetable oil may be pure cold-pressed rapeseed oil, sunflower oil, or a blend of corn, soya bean, rapeseed or other oils. It usually has a bland flavour and is suitable for stir-frying.

Spice mixes
Curry powder

Bought curry powders are readily available, but for optimum flavour make your own. To make your own curry powder:
Put 1 tbsp each cumin and fenugreek seeds, ½ tsp mustard seeds, 1½ tsp each poppy seeds, black peppercorns and ground ginger, 4 tbsp coriander seeds, ½ tsp hot chilli powder and 2 tbsp ground turmeric into an electric blender or grinder. Grind to a fine powder. Store the curry powder in an airtight container and use within one month.

Garam masala

Sold ready-prepared, this Indian spice mix is aromatic rather than hot. To make your own garam masala:
Grind together 10 green cardamom pods, 1 tbsp black peppercorns and 2 tsp cumin seeds. Store in an airtight container and use within one month.

Spicy Bean and Courgette Soup

Hands-on time: 10 minutes
Cooking time: 30 minutes

2 tbsp olive oil

175g (6oz) onions, finely chopped

2 garlic cloves, crushed

2 tsp ground coriander

1 tbsp paprika

1 tsp mild curry powder

450g (1lb) courgettes, trimmed, halved
and sliced

225g (8oz) potatoes, peeled and diced

400g can red kidney beans, drained
and rinsed

425g can flageolet beans, drained
and rinsed

1.5 litres (2½ pints) vegetable stock
(see page 13)

salt and freshly ground black pepper

crusty bread to serve

1 Heat the oil in a pan. Add the onions and garlic and sauté for 2 minutes. Add the spices and cook, stirring, for 1 minute. Mix in the courgettes and potatoes and cook for 1–2 minutes.

2 Add the remaining ingredients and bring to the boil, then reduce the heat, cover the pan and simmer for 25 minutes, stirring occasionally, or until the potatoes are tender. Adjust the seasoning if necessary.

3 Ladle into warmed bowls and serve with crusty bread.

Serves 4

Roasted Onion and Coconut Soup

Hands-on time: 25 minutes
Cooking time: 1 hour 40 minutes

4 large onions, about 1.1kg (2½lb), halved

2 tsp olive oil

3 large red chillies

6 garlic cloves, unpeeled

½ tsp cumin seeds

900ml (1½ pints) vegetable or chicken stock (see pages 13 and 14)

2 lemongrass stalks

3 kaffir lime leaves or zest of 1 small lime

2 × 400ml cans coconut milk

salt and freshly ground black pepper

For the Jamaican salsa

1 small banana (optional)

250g (8oz) plum tomatoes, quartered, seeded and finely chopped

1 green chilli, seeded and finely chopped (see page 78)

finely grated zest and juice of 1 lime

2 tbsp freshly chopped coriander

coriander, finely sliced red chilli and coconut milk to serve

1 Preheat the oven to 200°C (180°C fan oven) mark 6. Place the onions in a roasting tin and drizzle with oil. Cook for 20–30 minutes or until brown. Add the chillies, garlic and cumin seeds, cover with foil and cook for 40 minutes or until the onions are soft. Leave to cool.

2 Peel, halve and seed the chillies; discard the seeds. Squeeze the pulp from the garlic and discard the skins. Whiz the chillies, garlic and onions in a food processor until smooth. Transfer the purée to a pan, add the stock, lemongrass and lime leaves or lime zest and season to taste. Bring slowly to the boil, then reduce the heat, cover the pan and cook gently for 30 minutes.

3 For the salsa, peel the banana, if using, and chop into small pieces. Mix with the tomatoes, chilli, lime zest and juice and coriander.

4 Remove the lemongrass and lime leaves from the soup and discard. Stir in the coconut milk and heat gently. Ladle the soup into warmed bowls and add a spoonful of salsa, garnished with coriander, sliced chilli and a drizzle of coconut milk to each.

Serves 6

Curried Parsnip Soup

Hands-on time: 20 minutes
Cooking time: 50 minutes

40g (1½oz) butter

1 onion, sliced

700g (1½lb) parsnips, peeled, cored and finely diced

1 tsp curry powder

½ tsp ground cumin

1.2 litres (2 pints) chicken or vegetable stock (see pages 13 and 14)

150ml (¼ pint) single cream

salt and freshly ground black pepper

paprika to sprinkle

1 Melt the butter in a large pan. Add the onion and fry gently for 5–7 minutes. Add the parsnips and fry gently for about 3 minutes.

2 Stir in the curry powder and cumin and cook for a further 2 minutes.

3 Add the stock, season to taste with salt and ground black pepper and bring to the boil. Reduce the heat, cover the pan and simmer for 35 minutes or until the vegetables are tender.

4 Leave the soup to cool a little, then whiz in batches in a blender or food processor until smooth. Pour the soup back into the pan and adjust the seasoning. Add the cream and reheat but do not boil.

5 Ladle the soup into warmed bowls, sprinkle with paprika and serve.

Serves 6

Spiced Dal Soup

Hands-on time: 5 minutes
Cooking time: 1½ hours

125g (4oz) chana dal

1 tsp cumin seeds

2 tsp coriander seeds

1 tsp fenugreek seeds

3 dried red chillies

1 tbsp shredded coconut

2 tbsp ghee or polyunsaturated oil

225g (8oz) tomatoes, skinned and
    roughly chopped

½ tsp turmeric

1 tsp treacle

salt and freshly ground black pepper

fresh coriander sprigs to garnish

lemon wedges to serve

1 Pick over the dal and remove any grit or discoloured pulses. Put into a sieve and wash in cold running water, then drain well and put into a pan. Cover with 600ml (1 pint) water and bring to the boil, then reduce the heat, cover the pan and simmer for 1 hour or until tender.

2 Put the cumin, coriander, fenugreek, chillies and coconut into a small electric mill or blender and grind finely. Heat the ghee or oil in a heavy-based frying pan, add the spice mixture and fry, stirring, for 30 seconds. Whiz the dal to a purée in a blender or food processor and put into a pan. Stir in the remaining ingredients and 300ml (½ pint) water.

3 Bring to the boil, then reduce the heat, cover the pan and simmer for about 20 minutes. Taste and adjust the seasoning. Ladle into warmed bowls, garnish with coriander sprigs, and serve with lemon wedges to squeeze in.

Serves 4

Thai Chicken Broth

Hands-on time: 20 minutes
Cooking time: 25 minutes

1 tbsp olive oil

4 boneless skinless chicken thighs,
about 300g (11oz), shredded

3 garlic cloves, roughly chopped

2 red chillies, seeded and finely diced
(see page 78)

1 lemongrass stalk, finely sliced

5cm (2in) piece fresh root ginger, peeled
and finely chopped

150ml (¼ pint) white wine

1 litre (1¾ pints) chicken stock
(see page 14)

8 fresh coriander sprigs

50g (2oz) rice noodles

125g (4oz) green beans, trimmed
and halved

125g (4oz) bean sprouts

4 spring onions, finely sliced

2 tbsp Thai fish sauce (nam pla)

juice of ½ lime

salt and freshly ground black pepper

1 Heat the oil in a large pan over a
medium heat. Add the chicken, garlic,
chillies, lemongrass and ginger and
cook for 3–5 minutes until the chicken
is opaque.

2 Add the wine and bring to the boil,
then reduce the heat and simmer
until reduced by half. Add the stock
and bring to the boil. Reduce the heat
and simmer for 5 minutes or until the
chicken is cooked through.

3 Pick the leaves off the coriander and
put them to one side. Finely chop the
coriander stalks. Add the noodles to
the pan and cook for 1 minute, then
add the beans and coriander stalks.
Cook for 3 minutes.

4 Add the bean sprouts and spring
onions (putting a few to one side for
the garnish) along with the fish sauce
and lime juice. Heat through, then
taste for seasoning. Ladle the noodles
and broth into warmed bowls, making
sure each has some chicken and
bean sprouts. Garnish with coriander
leaves, spring onions and bean
sprouts and serve.

Serves 4

Perfect Chilli and Ginger

Most of a chilli's heat resides in the seeds and white pith, so it is usually best to remove these, then finely chop or slice the flesh with care. Fresh root ginger is one of the most frequently used wet spices and is easy to prepare.

Perfect chillies

1. Cut off the cap and slit open lengthways. Using a spoon, scrape out the seeds and the pith (the hottest parts of the chilli).
2. For diced chilli, cut into thin shreds lengthways, then cut crossways.

SAFETY TIP

Chillies vary enormously in strength, from quite mild to blisteringly hot, depending on the type of chilli and its ripeness. Taste a small piece first to check it's not too hot for you. Be extremely careful when handling chillies not to touch or rub your eyes with your fingers, as they will sting. Always wash your hands thoroughly with soap and water immediately after handling chillies. Wash knives immediately after handling chillies for the same reason. As a precaution, use rubber gloves when preparing them, if you like.

1

Perfect ginger

Grating

1 Cut off a piece of the root and peel with a vegetable peeler. Cut off any brown spots.
2 Rest the grater on a board or small plate and grate the ginger. Discard any large fibres adhering to the pulp.

Slicing, shredding and chopping

1 Cut slices off the ginger and cut off the skin carefully. Cut off any brown spots.
2 Stack the slices and cut into shreds. To chop, stack the shreds and cut across into small pieces.

Pressing

If you just need the ginger juice, peel and cut off any brown spots, then cut into small chunks and use a garlic press held over a small bowl to extract the juice.

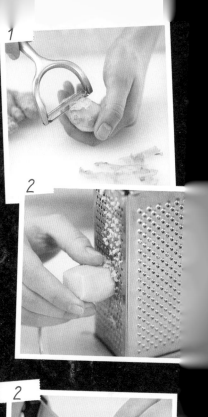

Hot and Sour Soup

Hands-on time: 20 minutes
Cooking time: 35 minutes

1 tbsp vegetable oil

2 turkey breasts, about 300g (11oz),
    or the same quantity of tofu, cut
    into strips

5cm (2in) piece fresh root ginger, peeled
    and grated

4 spring onions, finely sliced

1–2 tbsp Thai red curry paste

75g (3oz) long-grain wild rice

1.1 litres (2 pints) hot weak vegetable or
    chicken stock or boiling water (see
    pages 13 and 14)

200g (7oz) mangetouts, sliced

juice of 1 lime

4 tbsp roughly chopped fresh coriander
    to garnish

1 Heat the oil in a deep pan. Add
the turkey or tofu and cook over a
medium heat for 5 minutes or until
browned. Add the ginger and spring
onions and cook for a further 2–3
minutes. Stir in the curry paste
and cook for 1–2 minutes to warm
the spices.

2 Add the rice and stir to coat in the
curry paste. Pour the hot stock or
boiling water into the pan, stir once
and bring to the boil. Reduce the heat,
cover the pan and simmer for
20 minutes.

3 Add the mangetouts (putting a few to
one side for the garnish) and cook for
a further 5 minutes or until the rice is
cooked. Just before serving, squeeze
in the lime juice and stir to mix.

4 To serve, ladle into warmed bowls
and sprinkle with the coriander and
mangetout.

Serves 4

Vietnamese Turkey Noodle Soup

Hands-on time: 15 minutes
Cooking time: 10 minutes

1.8–2 litres (3¼–3½ pints) chicken stock
(see page 14)

4cm (1½in) fresh root ginger, peeled and
finely chopped

1 garlic clove, finely chopped

450g (1lb) turkey breast fillet, sliced into
thin strips

1 tbsp fish sauce

¼ head Savoy cabbage, finely shredded

100g (3½oz) rice noodles

a large handful of bean sprouts

juice of 1 lime

1 large red chilli, seeded and thinly
sliced (see page 78)

4 spring onions, sliced

salt and freshly ground black pepper

a large handful each of fresh coriander
and mint, roughly chopped, to garnish

1 Bring the stock to the boil in a large
pan. Add the ginger, garlic and turkey
and simmer for 5 minutes.

2 Stir in the fish sauce, cabbage and
noodles and cook for 3 minutes (check
the turkey is cooked). Add the bean
sprouts, lime juice and most of the
chilli and spring onions. Check the
seasoning. Divide among four bowls,
garnish with the herbs, remaining
chilli and spring onions. Serve
immediately.

Serves 4

Mulligatawny Soup

Hands-on time: 25 minutes
Cooking time: 40 minutes

3 rashers streaky bacon, rinded and finely chopped

550g (1¼lb) chicken portions

600ml (1 pint) hot chicken stock (see page 14)

1 carrot, sliced

1 celery stick, chopped

1 apple, cored and chopped

2 tsp curry powder

4 peppercorns, crushed

1 clove

1 bay leaf

1 tbsp plain flour

150ml (¼ pint) milk

50g (2oz) long-grain rice, cooked, and crusty bread to serve

1 Fry the bacon in a large pan until the fat begins to run. Do not allow the bacon to become brown.

2 Add the chicken and brown well. Drain the meat on kitchen paper and pour off the fat.

3 Put the bacon and chicken back into the pan and add the hot stock and the next seven ingredients. Cover the pan and simmer for about 30 minutes or until the chicken is tender.

4 Remove the chicken and leave to cool a little. Cut off the meat and put it back into the soup. Discard the clove and bay leaf and reheat the soup gently.

5 Mix the flour with a little cold water. Add to the soup with the milk and reheat without boiling.

6 Ladle the soup into four warmed bowls, spoon a mound of rice into each one and serve immediately with crusty bread.

Serves 4

Spicy Beef and Noodle Soup

Hands-on time: 10 minutes, plus soaking
Cooking time: 10 minutes

15g (½oz) dried porcini or shiitake
mushrooms

2 tbsp groundnut oil

225g (8oz) fillet steak, cut into thin strips

1.1 litres (2 pints) beef stock

2 tbsp Thai fish sauce (nam pla),
plus extra if needed

1 large fresh red chilli, seeded and finely
chopped (see page 78)

1 lemongrass stalk, trimmed and
thinly sliced

2.5cm (1in) piece of fresh root ginger,
peeled and finely chopped

6 spring onions, halved lengthways
and cut into 2.5cm (1in) lengths

1 garlic clove, crushed

¼ tsp caster sugar

50g (2oz) medium egg noodles

125g (4oz) fresh spinach leaves,
roughly chopped

4 tbsp freshly chopped coriander

freshly ground black pepper

1 Break the dried mushrooms into
pieces, and soak in 150ml (¼ pint)
boiling water for 15 minutes.

2 Meanwhile, heat the oil in a large
pan over a medium heat, brown the
meat in two batches and keep to one
side. Pour the stock into the pan with
2 tbsp fish sauce. Add the mushrooms
and their soaking liquor, the chilli,
lemongrass, ginger, spring onions,
garlic and sugar. Bring to the boil.

3 Break the noodles up slightly and
add to the pan, then stir gently until
they begin to separate. Reduce the
heat and simmer for 4–5 minutes until
the noodles are just tender, stirring
occasionally.

4 Stir in the spinach, coriander and
reserved steak. Check and adjust the
seasoning with ground black pepper,
and add a little more fish sauce if
necessary. Spoon into four warmed
bowls and serve hot.

Serves 4

Goulash Soup

Hands-on time: 20 minutes
Cooking time: about 2½ hours

700g (1½lb) silverside or lean chuck
   steak

25g (1oz) butter

225g (8oz) onions, chopped

1 small green pepper, seeded
   and chopped

4 tomatoes, skinned and quartered

150g (5oz) tomato purée

600ml (1 pint) rich beef stock

1 tbsp paprika

450g (1lb) potatoes, peeled

150ml (¼ pint) soured cream

salt and freshly ground black pepper

freshly chopped parsley to garnish
   (optional)

1 Wipe the meat with a damp cloth. Remove any excess fat or gristle and cut the meat into small pieces. Season well with 2 tsp salt and ground black pepper to taste.

2 Melt the butter in a large pan, add the onions and green pepper and sauté until tender.

3 Add the meat pieces, tomatoes, tomato purée, stock and paprika. Stir well and bring to the boil, then reduce the heat, cover the pan and simmer for 2½ hours, stirring occasionally.

4 Half an hour before the end of cooking, cut the potatoes into bite-size pieces, bring to the boil in lightly salted water, reduce the heat and simmer until cooked. Drain well and add to the soup.

5 Check the seasoning and stir in 2 tbsp soured cream. Ladle into warmed bowls, garnish with chopped parsley, if you like, and serve the remaining soured cream separately, for each person to spoon into their soup.

Serves 6

Lamb, Lentil and Chilli Soup

Hands-on time: 15 minutes
Cooking time: about 1 hour 40 minutes

1 tbsp vegetable oil

350g (12oz) lamb neck fillet, cut into small cubes

1 onion, finely chopped

2 medium carrots, finely chopped

1 celery stick, finely chopped

1 tsp ground cumin

1 tsp ground coriander

300g (11oz) yellow split peas

1.3 litres (2¼ pints) vegetable stock (see page 13)

1 bay leaf

salt and freshly ground black pepper

crusty bread to serve

To garnish

2 tbsp natural yogurt

1 red chilli, seeded and sliced into rings (see page 78)

a small handful of fresh parsley or coriander leaves, chopped

1 Heat the oil in a large pan over a medium heat and fry the lamb until nicely browned (do this in batches if necessary to stop the meat sweating). Lift the lamb out of the pan and put to one side, leaving as much oil in the pan as possible.

2 Add the chopped vegetables to the pan and cook for 5 minutes or until softened. Stir in the spices and fry for 2 minutes more. Put the lamb back into the pan with the split peas, stock and bay leaf. Bring to the boil, then reduce the heat, cover and simmer for about 1 hour 20 minutes, stirring/mashing it occasionally, until the lamb is tender and the mixture has cooked down to a fairly smooth soup.

3 Check the seasoning, adjust the consistency if you like with more stock or water and ladle into warmed bowls. Garnish with a swirl of yogurt, some fresh chilli and chopped herbs and serve with crusty bread.

Serves 4

Feel-good Soups

Red Lentil Soup with Low-fat Cornbread

Hands-on time: 30 minutes
Cooking time: about 30 minutes

1 tsp extra virgin olive oil, plus extra
    to drizzle (optional)

1 onion, roughly chopped

2 celery sticks, roughly chopped

1 garlic clove, chopped

1 tsp chilli powder (or to taste)

250g (9oz) red lentils, washed

400g can chopped tomatoes

1.1 litres (2 pints) vegetable stock
    (see page 13)

For the cornbread
(cuts into 8 slices)

100g (3½oz) plain flour

100g (3½oz) quick-cook polenta

1 tbsp caster sugar

½ tsp bicarbonate of soda

1 medium egg

175g (6oz) low-fat natural yogurt

salt

1 Start by making the soup. Heat the oil in a large pan. Add the onion and celery and gently cook for 10 minutes until softened. Stir in the garlic and chilli powder and cook for 1 minute. Add the lentils, tomatoes and stock and bring to the boil, then reduce the heat and simmer gently for 15 minutes or until the lentils are tender.

2 Meanwhile, make the cornbread. Preheat the oven to 180°C (160°C fan oven) mark 4 and line a 450g (1lb) loaf tin with baking parchment. Measure the flour, polenta, sugar and soda into a large bowl. Add ½–¾ tsp salt (depending on taste) and whisk to combine.

3 In a separate jug, whisk together the egg and yogurt. Add to the dry ingredients and whisk until just combined. Scrape into the prepared tin, level the surface and bake for 20–25 minutes until golden and firm

to the touch. Leave to rest in the tin for 10 minutes.

4 Blend the soup until smooth (do this in batches if necessary) and pour back into the pan. Check the seasoning (if the soup is too thick for your liking, add a little more water).

5 To serve, reheat the soup (if necessary), then ladle into warmed bowls and drizzle with oil, if you like. Serve with the warm sliced cornbread.

Serves 4

Spiced Cauliflower Soup

Hands-on time: 15 minutes
Cooking time: 35 minutes

1 tbsp chilli oil, plus extra to drizzle
  (optional)

1 medium onion, chopped

1 garlic clove, crushed

2 tsp ground coriander

1 medium cauliflower, cut into florets

1 large potato, peeled and cubed

1 lemon

1.4 litres (2½ pints) hot chicken stock
  (see page 14)

2 tsp extra virgin olive oil

6 tsp natural yogurt

salt and freshly ground black pepper

25g (1oz) flaked almonds, toasted,
  to garnish

1 Heat the chilli oil in a large pan. Add the onion and gently fry for 10 minutes or until softened. Add a little salt to the pan now – it gives extra depth of flavour to the soup. Add the garlic and coriander and fry for 2 minutes. Stir in the cauliflower and potato and cook for 3 minutes.

2 Zest the lemon and add the zest to the pan with the hot stock. Season and bring to the boil, then reduce the heat, cover and simmer for 15–20 minutes until the vegetables are tender. Leave to cool a little then whiz the soup in batches in a blender until smooth.

3 Pour the soup back into the rinsed-out pan. Reheat gently and check the seasoning. Divide among six warmed bowls.

4 Juice half the lemon and mix with the olive oil. Swirl 1 tsp yogurt into each bowl. Drizzle with the lemon oil and some extra chilli oil, if you like, then garnish with the almonds. Serve immediately.

SAVE TIME

Prepare the soup to the end of step 2. Chill for up to two days. Complete the recipe to serve.

Serves 6

Full-of-goodness Soup

Hands-on time: 10 minutes
Cooking time: about 8 minutes

1–2 tbsp medium curry paste

200ml (7fl oz) reduced-fat coconut milk

600ml (1 pint) hot vegetable stock
(see page 13)

200g (7oz) smoked tofu, cubed

2 pak choi, chopped

a handful of sugarsnap peas

4 spring onions, chopped

lime wedges to serve

1 Heat the curry paste in a pan for 1–2 minutes. Add the coconut milk and hot stock and bring to the boil.
2 Add the tofu, pak choi, sugarsnap peas and spring onions, then reduce the heat and simmer for 1–2 minutes.
3 Ladle into warmed bowls and serve each with a wedge of lime to squeeze over the soup.

Serves 4

Perfect Onions and Peppers

Onions

1. Cut off the tip and base of the onion. Peel away all the layers of papery skin and any discoloured layers underneath.
2. Put the onion root end down on the chopping board, then, using a sharp knife, cut the onion in half from tip to base.

Slicing

Put one half on the board with the cut surface facing down and slice across the onion.

Chopping

Slice the halved onions from the root end to the top at regular intervals. Next, make two or three horizontal slices through the onion, then slice vertically across the width.

Seeding peppers

The seeds and white pith of peppers taste bitter, so should be removed.

1 Cut off the top of the pepper, then cut away and discard the seeds and white pith.

2 Alternatively, cut the pepper in half vertically and snap out the white pithy core and seeds. Trim away the rest of the white membrane with a knife.

1

Roasted Tomato and Pepper Soup

Hands-on time: 20 minutes
Cooking time: about 1 hour

1.4kg (3lb) full-flavoured tomatoes, preferably vine-ripened
2 red peppers, seeded and chopped
4 garlic cloves, crushed
3 small onions, thinly sliced
20g (¾oz) fresh thyme sprigs
4 tbsp olive oil
4 tbsp Worcestershire sauce
4 tbsp vodka
salt and freshly ground black pepper
6 tbsp double cream to serve

1 Preheat the oven to 200°C (180°C fan oven) mark 6. Put the tomatoes into a large roasting tin with the peppers, garlic and onions. Scatter six of the thyme sprigs over the top, drizzle with oil and roast in the oven for 25 minutes. Turn the vegetables over and roast for a further 30–40 minutes until tender and slightly charred.

2 Put one-third of the vegetables into a blender or food processor with 300ml (½ pint) boiled water. Add the Worcestershire sauce and vodka and season with salt and ground black pepper. Whiz in a blender until smooth, then pass through a sieve into a pan.

3 Whiz the remaining vegetables with 450ml (¾ pint) boiled water, then sieve and add to the pan.

4 To serve, warm the soup thoroughly, stirring occasionally. Ladle into warmed bowls, add 1 tbsp double cream to each bowl, then drag a cocktail stick through the cream to swirl. Scatter a few fresh thyme leaves over the top and serve immediately.

Serves 6

Panzanella Soup

Hands-on time: 20 minutes
Cooking time: 15 minutes

1 red onion, finely chopped

2 garlic cloves, crushed

2 red peppers, seeded and
  roughly chopped

1 cucumber, peeled, seeded and
  roughly chopped

1 tbsp olive oil, plus extra to garnish

125g (4oz) wholemeal bread, cut into
  2cm (¾in) cubes

400g can chopped tomatoes

750ml (1¼ pints) vegetable stock
  (see page 13)

a large handful of fresh basil

salt and freshly ground black pepper

black olives, pitted and sliced, and
  capers to garnish (optional)

croûtons to serve

1 Put the onion, garlic, red peppers
  and cucumber into a large pan with a
  splash of water. Cook gently for about
  10 minutes until softened (add a
  little water as needed).

2 Meanwhile, heat the oil in a separate
  large frying pan over a low-medium
  heat. Add the bread cubes and some
  salt. Cook, tossing occasionally, until
  golden. Put to one side.

3 Add tomatoes, stock, most of the basil
  and some seasoning to the vegetable
  pan. Simmer for 5 minutes, then whiz
  the soup (in batches if necessary) until
  smooth. Check the seasoning.

4 Reheat, if needed, and pour into four
  warmed bowls. Garnish with the
  olives, capers, oil and remaining basil,
  if you like. Serve with croûtons.

FREEZE AHEAD

To make ahead and freeze, prepare the
soup to end of step 3 (without making
the croûtons). Cool, chill and pack into
a freezerproof bag. Freeze for up to six
months. To serve, thaw, then reheat
gently in a pan. Make the croûtons
and complete the recipe to serve.

Perfect Herbs

Most herbs are the leaf of a flowering plant and are usually sold with much of the stalk intact. They have to be washed, trimmed and then chopped or torn into pieces suitable for your recipe.

Washing

1. Trim the roots and part of the stalks from the herbs. Immerse in a bowl of cold water and shake briskly. Leave in the water for a few minutes.
2. Lift out of the water and put into a colander or sieve, then rinse again under cold water. Leave to drain for a few minutes, then dry thoroughly on kitchen paper or teatowels, or use a salad spinner.

1

- ❑ Don't pour the herbs and their water into the sieve, because dirt in the water might get caught in the leaves
- ❑ If the herb has fleshy stalks, such as parsley or coriander, the stalks can be saved to flavour stock or soup. Tie them in a bundle with kitchen string for easy removal

Chopping

1 Trim the herbs by pinching off all but the smallest, most tender stalks. If the herb is one with a woody stalk, such as rosemary or thyme, it may be easier to remove the leaves by rubbing the whole bunch between your hands; the leaves should simply pull off the stems.

2 If you are chopping the leaves, gather them into a compact ball in one hand, keeping your fist around the ball (but being careful not to crush them).

3 Chop with a large knife, using a rocking motion and letting just a little of the ball out of your fingers at a time.

4 When the herbs are roughly chopped, continue chopping until the pieces are in small shreds or flakes.

Herb and Lemon Soup

Hands-on time: 10 minutes
Cooking time: 15 minutes

1.7 litres (3 pints) chicken stock
  (see page 14)
150g (5oz) orzo or other dried soup pasta
3 medium eggs
juice of 1 large lemon
2 tbsp finely chopped fresh chives
2 tbsp finely chopped fresh chervil
salt and freshly ground black pepper
lemon wedges to serve

1 Bring the stock to the boil in a large pan. Add the pasta and cook for 5 minutes or according to the packet instructions.
2 Beat the eggs in a bowl until frothy, then add the lemon juice and 1 tbsp cold water. Slowly stir in two ladlefuls of the hot stock. Put the egg mixture into the pan with the rest of the stock, then warm through over a very low heat for 2–3 minutes.
3 Add the chives and chervil and season with salt and ground black pepper. Ladle the soup into warmed bowls and serve immediately, with lemon wedges.

Serves 6

Celery Soup

Hands-on time: 10 minutes
Cooking time: 40 minutes

25g (1oz) butter

1 tbsp olive oil

1 medium leek, trimmed and sliced

6 celery sticks, finely sliced

1 tbsp finely chopped sage

600ml (1 pint) hot chicken stock
(see page 14)

300ml (½ pint) milk

salt and freshly ground black pepper

fresh basil sprigs to garnish

1 Melt the butter in a pan and add the oil. Add the leek and fry for 10–15 minutes until soft. Add the celery and sage and cook for 5 minutes to soften.

2 Add the hot stock and milk to the pan, then season with salt and ground black pepper, cover and bring to the boil. Reduce the heat and simmer for 10–15 minutes until the celery is tender.

3 Leave the soup to cool a little, then whiz in batches in a blender or food processor until smooth. Pour the soup back into the pan, reheat gently and season with salt and ground black pepper.

4 Ladle into warmed bowls, sprinkle with black pepper, garnish with basil sprigs and serve.

Serves 4

Healing Chicken and Ginger Broth

Hands-on time: 15 minutes
Cooking time: 10 minutes

3 × 125g (4oz) skinless chicken breasts, cut into strips

1.4 litres (2½ pints) strong chicken stock (see page 14)

4cm (1½in) fresh root ginger, peeled and cut into matchsticks

½–1 red chilli, seeded and finely sliced (see page 78)

125g pack baby sweetcorn, chopped

2 large carrots, cut into matchsticks

200g (7oz) uncooked egg noodles or 250g (8oz) cooked rice

4 spring onions, finely sliced

small handful of fresh parsley, finely chopped, to garnish

SAVE MONEY

If you have any leftover roast chicken, use this instead of poaching chicken specially for this soup. Simply add to the simmering stock to warm through for a quick, economical supper.

1 Put the chicken in a medium pan and cover with cold water. Bring to the boil, reduce the heat and simmer gently for 5 minutes or until cooked through.

2 Meanwhile, in a large pan, bring the stock to the boil and add the ginger and chilli. Reduce the heat and simmer for a few minutes, then add the sweetcorn, carrots, noodles or rice and most of the spring onions. Simmer for 3 minutes until the noodles, if using, are cooked and the vegetables are just softening.

3 Drain the cooked chicken and divide among four soup bowls. Ladle over the stock mixture, sprinkle over the remaining spring onions and the parsley and serve.

Serves 4

Healthy Fish Chowder

Hands-on time: 20 minutes
Cooking time: 25 minutes

1 tbsp olive oil

1 onion, finely chopped

1 celery stick, finely chopped

500ml (18fl oz) hot vegetable or fish stock (see pages 13 and 14)

250ml (9fl oz) skimmed milk

200g (7oz) baby new potatoes, halved

150g (5oz) skinless smoked haddock, diced

150g (5oz) skinless white fish, such as cod or pollack, diced

2 × 198g cans sweetcorn, drained

2 tbsp double cream

2 tbsp freshly chopped chives

salt and freshly ground black pepper

1 Heat the oil in a large pan over a medium heat. Add the onion and celery and gently fry for about 10 minutes until soft and translucent.

2 Add the hot stock and milk, then bring to the boil. Add the potatoes, then reduce the heat and simmer for 10 minutes or until the vegetables are tender.

3 Stir in the fish, sweetcorn and some seasoning and simmer for 3–5 minutes until the fish is cooked. Carefully stir through the cream and most of the chives and check the seasoning. Garnish with the remaining chives and serve.

Comfort Soups

Keep It Seasonal

Why? Because not only will the produce you buy taste fantastic, it will also cost less. Look out for good deals at supermarkets, farm shops, markets and greengrocers, where you can sometimes buy larger, cheaper quantities for freezing or batch cooking. Pick Your Own farms often charge half the price of the supermarkets. You can pick fruit and vegetables at their ripest and enjoy a fun day out with the family too.

January

Vegetables Beetroot, Brussels sprouts, cauliflower, celeriac, celery, chicory, Jerusalem artichokes, kale, leeks, parsnips, potatoes (maincrop), rhubarb, swede, turnips

Fruit Apples, clementines, kiwi fruit, lemons, oranges, passion fruit, pears, pineapple, pomegranate, satsumas, tangerines, walnuts

Fish Clams, cockles, haddock, hake, lemon sole, mussels, plaice

February

Vegetables Brussels sprouts, cauliflower, celeriac, chicory, kale, leeks, parsnips, potatoes (maincrop), rhubarb, swede

Fruit Bananas, blood oranges, kiwi fruit, lemons, oranges, passion fruit, pears, pineapple, pomegranate

Fish Cockles, cod, haddock, hake, lemon sole, mussels, salmon

March

Vegetables Cauliflower, chicory, kale, leeks, purple sprouting broccoli, rhubarb, spring onions
Fruit Bananas, blood oranges, kiwi fruit, lemons, oranges, passion fruit, pineapple, pomegranate
Fish Cockles, cod, hake, lemon sole, mussels, salmon, sea trout

April

Vegetables Asparagus, broccoli, Jersey royal potatoes, purple sprouting broccoli, radishes, rhubarb, rocket, spinach, spring onions, watercress
Fruit Bananas, kiwi fruit
Fish Cockles, cod, salmon, sea trout

May

Vegetables Asparagus, broccoli, Jersey royal potatoes, new potatoes, radishes, rhubarb, rocket, spinach, spring onions, watercress
Fruit Cherries, kiwi fruit, strawberries
Meat Lamb
Fish Cod, crab, lemon sole, plaice, salmon, sea bass, sea trout

June

Vegetables Artichokes, asparagus, aubergines, broad beans, broccoli, carrots, courgettes, fennel, mangetouts, Jersey royal potatoes, new potatoes, peas, radishes, rocket, runner beans, spring onions, turnips, watercress
Fruit Cherries, strawberries
Meat Lamb
Fish Cod, crab, haddock, herring, lemon sole, mackerel, plaice, salmon, sardines, sea bass, sea trout

July

Vegetables Artichokes, aubergines, beetroot, broad beans, broccoli, carrots, courgettes, cucumber, fennel, French beans, garlic, mangetouts, new potatoes, onions, peas, potatoes (maincrop), radishes, rocket, runner beans, turnips, watercress
Fruit Apricots, blackberries, blueberries, cherries, gooseberries, greengages, kiwi fruit, melons, peaches, raspberries, redcurrants, strawberries, tomatoes
Meat Lamb, rabbit
Fish Cod, crab, haddock, herring, lemon sole, mackerel, plaice, salmon, sardines, sea bass, sea trout

August

Vegetables Artichokes, aubergines, beetroot, broad beans, broccoli, carrots, courgettes, cucumber, fennel, French beans, garlic, leeks, mangetouts, marrow, new potatoes, onions, peas, peppers, potatoes (maincrop), radishes, rocket, runner beans, sweetcorn, watercress

Fruit Apricots, blackberries, blueberries, damsons, greengages, kiwi fruit, melons, nectarines, peaches, plums, raspberries, redcurrants, tomatoes

Meat Lamb, rabbit

Fish Cod, crab, grey mullet, haddock, herring, lemon sole, mackerel, plaice, salmon, sardines, sea bass

September

Vegetables Artichokes, aubergines, beetroot, broccoli, butternut squash, carrots, courgettes, cucumber, fennel, garlic, leeks, mangetouts, marrow, onions, parsnips, peas, peppers, potatoes (maincrop), radishes, rocket, runner beans, sweetcorn, watercress, wild mushrooms

Fruit Apples, blackberries, damsons, figs, grapes, melons, nectarines, peaches, pears, plums, raspberries, redcurrants, tomatoes, walnuts

Meat Lamb, rabbit

Fish Clams, cod, crab, grey mullet, haddock, herring, lemon sole, mackerel, plaice, sea bass, squid

October

Vegetables Artichokes, beetroot, broccoli, butternut squash, carrots, celeriac, celery, fennel, kale, leeks, marrow, onions, parsnips, potatoes (maincrop), pumpkin, swede, turnips, watercress, wild mushrooms

Fruit Apples, chestnuts, figs, pears, quince, tomatoes, walnuts

Meat Rabbit

Fish Brill, clams, crab, grey mullet, haddock, hake, lemon sole, mackerel, mussels, plaice, sea bass, squid

November

Vegetables Artichokes, beetroot, Brussels sprouts, celeriac, celery, chicory, kale, leeks, parsnips, potatoes (maincrop), pumpkin, swede, turnips, watercress, wild mushrooms

Fruit Apples, chestnuts, clementines, cranberries, figs, passion fruit, pears, quince, satsumas, tangerines, walnuts

Meat Rabbit

Fish Brill, clams, haddock, hake, lemon sole, mussels, plaice, sea bass, squid

December

Vegetables Beetroot, Brussels sprouts, cauliflower, celeriac, celery, chicory, kale, leeks, parsnips, potatoes (maincrop), pumpkin, swede, turnips

Fruit Apples, chestnuts, clementines, cranberries, passion fruit, pears, pineapple, pomegranate, satsumas, tangerines, walnuts

Meat Rabbit

Fish Brill, clams, haddock, hake, lemon sole, mussels, plaice, sea bass

Green Chicken Curry Soup

Hands-on time: 20 minutes
Cooking time: about 25 minutes

1 garlic clove

4 spring onions, roughly chopped

3cm (1¼in) piece fresh root ginger, peeled

1 green chilli, seeded and roughly chopped (see page 78)

75g (3oz) fresh coriander, plus extra to garnish

400ml (14fl oz) coconut milk

1 tbsp vegetable oil

750ml (1¼ pint) hot chicken stock (see page 14)

600g (1lb 5oz) skinless chicken thigh fillets, sliced into strips

175g (6oz) baby sweetcorn, roughly chopped

200g (7oz) sugarsnap peas, roughly chopped

1 tbsp fish sauce

1 tbsp soy sauce

lime wedges to serve

1 Whiz the garlic, spring onions, ginger, chilli, coriander and coconut milk in a blender until smooth. Heat the oil in a large pan over a medium heat and add the blended coconut mixture. Bring to the boil, then add the hot stock and chicken strips. Reduce the heat and simmer for 15 minutes or until chicken is cooked through.

2 Use a slotted spoon to lift out roughly half the chicken pieces and put to one side. Blend the remaining soup (you may need to do this in batches) until smooth, then pour back into the rinsed-out pan. Add the reserved chicken, chopped sweetcorn and sugarsnap peas, and the fish sauce.

3 Heat through and simmer just until the vegetables are tender. Check the seasoning, then drizzle on the soy sauce and garnish with a little extra coriander. Serve with lime wedges on the side.

Serves 4

Chicken and Dumpling Soup

Hands-on time: 20 minutes
Cooking time: 25 minutes

1½ tbsp olive oil

1 medium onion, finely chopped

2 carrots, finely diced

3 celery sticks, finely diced

1 garlic clove, crushed

1.6 litres (2¾ pints) chicken stock (see page 14)

500g (1lb 2oz) skinless chicken thigh fillets, cut into finger-size strips

1 leek, trimmed and sliced into rings

100g (3½oz) plain flour

½ tsp baking powder

a large handful of fresh parsley, chopped

5 tbsp semi-skimmed milk

salt and freshly ground black pepper

1 Heat ½ tbsp of the oil in a pan. Add the onion, carrots and celery and fry for 10 minutes until softened. Stir in the garlic and cook for 1 minute.

2 Pour in the stock and bring to the boil. Add the chicken and leek, bring back to the boil, reduce the heat and simmer for 6 minutes or until the chicken is cooked and the vegetables are just tender.

3 Meanwhile, put the flour into a medium bowl. Stir in the baking powder, some of the parsley and plenty of seasoning. Add the remaining oil and milk and stir together until just combined to make a rough, slightly sticky dough.

4 Drop small teaspoonfuls of the dumpling mixture into the simmering stock and cook for 4 minutes (the dumplings will swell up, so don't make them too big). Check the seasoning.

5 Ladle the soup and dumplings into warmed soup bowls, garnish with the remaining parsley and serve.

Serves 6

Cock-a-leekie Soup

Hands-on time: 30–40 minutes
Cooking time: 1 hour 20 minutes

1 oven-ready chicken, about 1.4kg (3lb)

2 onions, roughly chopped

2 carrots, roughly chopped

2 celery sticks, roughly chopped

1 bay leaf

25g (1oz) butter

900g (2lb) leeks, trimmed and sliced

125g (4oz) ready to eat stoned prunes, sliced

salt and freshly ground black pepper

freshly chopped parsley to serve

For the dumplings

125g (4oz) self-raising white flour

a pinch of salt

50g (2oz) shredded suet

2 tbsp freshly chopped parsley

2 tbsp freshly chopped thyme

1 Put the chicken into a pan in which it fits quite snugly. Add the chopped vegetables, bay leaf and chicken giblets (if available). Add 1.7 litres (3 pints) water and bring to the boil, then reduce the heat, cover the pan and simmer gently for 1 hour.

2 Meanwhile, melt the butter in a large pan. Add the leeks and fry gently for 10 minutes or until softened.

3 Remove the chicken from the pan. Strain the stock and put to one side. Strip the chicken from the bones and shred roughly. Add to the stock with the prunes and softened leeks.

4 To make the dumplings, sift the flour and salt into a bowl. Stir in the suet, herbs and about 5 tbsp water to make a fairly firm dough. Lightly shape the dough into 2.5cm (1in) balls. Bring the soup just to the boil and season well. Reduce the heat, add the dumplings and cover the pan with a lid. Simmer for about 15–20 minutes until the dumplings are light and fluffy. Serve scattered with chopped parsley.

Serves 8

Turkey, Sprout and Chestnut Soup

Hands-on time: 5 minutes
Cooking time: 45 minutes

25g (1oz) butter or margarine

1 large onion, chopped

225g (8oz) Brussels sprouts

900ml (1½ pints) turkey stock made
from leftover carcass and any
leftover turkey meat

400g can whole chestnuts, drained

2 tsp freshly chopped thyme or
1 tsp dried thyme

stock or milk to finish

salt and freshly ground black pepper

fresh thyme sprigs to garnish

crusty bread to serve

1 Melt the butter or margarine in a
large heavy-based pan, add the onion
and fry gently for 5 minutes until it
has softened.

2 Trim the sprouts and cut a cross in the
base of each one. Add to the onion,
cover the pan with a lid and cook
gently for 5 minutes, shaking the
pan frequently.

3 Pour in the stock and bring to the boil,
then add the remaining ingredients,
with salt and ground black pepper to
taste. Reduce the heat, cover the pan
and simmer for 30 minutes until the
vegetables are tender.

4 Leave the soup to cool a little, then
whiz in batches in a blender or food
processor until smooth. Pour back into
the rinsed-out pan and reheat gently,
then thin down with either stock or
milk, according to taste.

5 Taste and adjust the seasoning.
Ladle into warmed bowls and garnish
with thyme. Serve with crusty bread.

Serves 4

London Particular

Hands-on time: 10 minutes
Cooking time: 1 hour 20 minutes

15g (½oz) butter

50g (2oz) streaky bacon rashers, rind removed, chopped

1 onion, roughly chopped

1 carrot, diced

1 celery stick, chopped

450g (1lb) split dried peas

2.3 litres (4 pints) chicken or ham stock (see page 14)

4 tbsp natural yogurt

salt and freshly ground black pepper

chopped grilled bacon and croûtons to garnish

1 Melt the butter in a large pan. Add the bacon, onion, carrot and celery and cook for 5–10 minutes until beginning to soften.

2 Add the peas and stock and bring to the boil, then cover, reduce the heat and simmer for 1 hour until the peas are soft.

3 Leave to cool slightly, then whiz in batches in a blender or food processor until smooth.

4 Pour the soup back into the pan. Season to taste with salt and ground black pepper, add the yogurt and reheat gently. Serve hot, garnished with bacon and croûtons.

Serves 8

Perfect Mussels

One of the most popular shellfish, mussels take moments to cook.
Careful preparation is important, so give yourself enough time to
get the shellfish ready.

Storing mussels

To store fresh mussels safely,
keep in an open bag in the fridge,
covered lightly with damp kitchen
paper (do not submerge in water
for prolonged periods of time).
Before use, check to make sure
the mussels are alive – the shells
should be tightly closed (give them
a sharp tap on a worksurface if they
aren't, and discard any that haven't
closed after 30 seconds or any that
have broken shells).

Preparing mussels

1 Scrape off the fibres attached
   to the shells (beards). If the
   mussels are very clean, give
   them a quick rinse under the
   cold tap. If they are very sandy,
   scrub them with a stiff brush.

2 If the shells have sizeable
   barnacles on them, it is best
   (though not essential) to remove
   them. Rap them sharply with
   a metal spoon or the back of
   a washing-up brush, then
   scrape off.

Cooking mussels

1. Discard any open mussels that don't shut when sharply tapped; this means they are dead and could be dangerous to eat.

2. In a large heavy-based pan, fry 2 finely chopped shallots and a generous handful of parsley in 25g (1oz) butter for about 2 minutes or until soft. Pour in 1cm (½in) dry white wine.

3. Add the mussels to the pan and cover tightly with a lid. Steam for 5–10 minutes until the shells open. Immediately take the pan away from the heat.

4. Using a slotted spoon, remove the mussels from the pan and discard any that haven't opened, then boil the cooking liquid rapidly to reduce. Pour over the mussels and serve immediately.

Hearty Mussel Soup

Hands-on time: 25 minutes
Cooking time: 20 minutes

1kg (2lb 2oz) fresh mussels
  (see page 132)

1 tbsp olive oil

2 onions, finely chopped

1 leek, finely sliced

3 large carrots, diced

2 medium potatoes, cut into small cubes

2 garlic cloves, crushed

1 bay leaf

900ml (1½ pint) vegetable or fish stock
  (see pages 13 and 14)

50ml (2fl oz) double cream

salt and freshly ground black pepper

2 tbsp chopped fresh chives to garnish

crusty bread to serve

1 Sort the mussels and clean, removing the barnacles and beards with a knife. Heat a large pan and add the mussels. Cover and cook for 3–4 minutes until mussels open. Strain. Put a few in their shells to one side; pick out the meat from the rest. Discard the empty shells and mussels that haven't opened.

2 Heat the oil in a large pan. Add the onions, leek, carrots and potatoes and gently cook for 10 minutes until tender. Stir in the garlic and bay leaf and cook for 1 minute. Pour in the stock and bring to the boil.

3 Add the mussel meat and cream. Discard the bay leaf and check the seasoning. Divide among four warmed soup bowls, scatter over the chopped chives and garnish with the reserved mussels in shells. Serve with crusty bread.

Serves 4

Smoked Cod and Sweetcorn Chowder

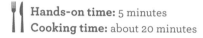

🍴 **Hands-on time:** 5 minutes
Cooking time: about 20 minutes

130g pack cubed pancetta

50g (2oz) butter

3 leeks, about 450g (1lb), trimmed and thinly sliced

25g (1oz) plain flour

600ml (1 pint) semi-skimmed or full-fat milk

700g (1½lb) undyed smoked cod loin or haddock, skinned and cut into 2cm (¾in) cubes

326g can sweetcorn in water, drained

450g (1lb) small new potatoes, sliced

150ml (¼ pint) double cream

½ tsp paprika

salt and freshly ground black pepper

2 tbsp freshly chopped flat-leafed parsley to garnish

1 Fry the pancetta in a large pan over a gentle heat until the fat runs out. Add the butter to the pan to melt, then add the leeks and cook until softened.

2 Stir in the flour and cook for a few seconds, then pour in the milk and 300ml (½ pint) cold water. Add the fish to the pan with the sweetcorn and potatoes. Bring to the boil, then reduce the heat and simmer for 10–15 minutes until the potatoes are cooked.

3 Stir in the cream, season with salt and pepper and the paprika and cook for 2–3 minutes to warm through. Ladle into warmed shallow bowls and sprinkle each one with a little chopped parsley. Serve immediately.

Serves 6

Cullen Skink

Hands-on time: 10 minutes
Cooking time: 1½ hours

1 Finnan haddock, weighing about 350g (12oz), skinned
1 medium onion, chopped
600ml (1 pint) milk
700g (1½lb) potatoes, peeled and chopped
a knob of butter
salt and freshly ground black pepper
freshly chopped flat-leafed parsley to garnish
crusty bread to serve

1 Put the haddock into a medium pan, just cover it with about 900ml (1½ pints) boiling water and bring to the boil again. Add the onion, cover and simmer for 10–15 minutes until the haddock is tender. Drain off the liquid and put to one side.

2 Remove the bones from the haddock and flake the flesh, then put to one side. Put the bones and strained stock back into the pan with the milk. Cover and simmer gently for a further hour.

3 Meanwhile, cook the potatoes in lightly salted boiling water until tender. Drain well, then mash.

4 Strain the liquid from the bones and put it back into the pan with the flaked fish. Add the mashed potato and the butter and stir well to give a thick creamy consistency. Adjust the seasoning and garnish with parsley. Serve with crusty bread.

Serves 4

Mexican Bean Soup

Hands-on time: 15 minutes
Cooking time: 25 minutes

4 tbsp olive oil

1 onion, chopped

2 garlic cloves, chopped

a pinch of crushed dried red chillies

1 tsp ground coriander

1 tsp ground cumin

½ tsp ground cinnamon

900ml (1½ pints) hot vegetable stock
(see page 13)

300ml (½ pint) tomato juice

1–2 tsp chilli sauce

2 × 400g cans red kidney beans

2 tbsp freshly chopped coriander

salt and freshly ground black pepper

fresh coriander leaves to garnish

crusty bread and lime butter to serve
(optional, see below)

Lime Butter

Beat the grated zest and juice of
½ lime into 50g (2oz) softened butter
and season to taste. Shape into a log,
wrap in clingfilm and chill until needed.
To serve, unwrap and slice thinly.

1 Heat the oil in a large pan. Add the
onion, garlic, chillies and spices
and fry gently for 5 minutes or until
lightly golden.

2 Add the hot stock, the tomato juice,
chilli sauce and beans with their
liquid. Bring to the boil, then reduce
the heat, cover the pan and simmer
gently for 20 minutes.

3 Leave the soup to cool a little, then
whiz in batches in a blender or
food processor until very smooth.
Return the soup to the pan, stir in the
chopped coriander and heat through,
then season to taste with salt and
ground black pepper.

4 Ladle the soup into warmed bowls.
Top each portion with a few slices
of lime butter, if you like, and scatter
with torn coriander leaves. Serve
with crusty bread and more lime
butter, if you like.

Pepper and Lentil Soup

Hands-on time: 15 minutes
Cooking time: 50 minutes

1 tbsp oil

1 medium onion, finely chopped

1 celery stick, chopped

1 leek, trimmed and chopped

1 carrot, chopped

2 red peppers, seeded and diced

225g (8oz) red lentils, washed

400g can chopped tomatoes

1 litre (1¾ pints) hot light vegetable stock (see page 13)

25g pack flat-leafed parsley, chopped

salt and freshly ground black pepper

toast to serve

1 Heat the oil in a pan. Add the onion, celery, leek and carrot and cook for 10–15 minutes until soft.

2 Add the red peppers and cook for 5 minutes. Stir in the red lentils, add the tomatoes and hot stock and season to taste with salt and ground black pepper.

3 Cover the pan and bring to the boil, then reduce the heat and cook, uncovered, for 25 minutes until the lentils are soft and the vegetables are tender.

4 Stir in the parsley. Ladle into warmed bowls and serve with toast.

Serves 6

Pasta and Chickpea Soup with Pesto

Hands-on time: 25 minutes
Cooking time: about 1 hour

3 tbsp olive oil

1 onion, chopped

2 garlic cloves, finely chopped

1 small leek, trimmed and sliced

1 tsp freshly chopped rosemary

400g can chickpeas

1.2 litres (2 pints) vegetable stock
   (see page 13)

4 ripe tomatoes, skinned and chopped

1 courgette, diced

125g (4oz) shelled peas

125g (4oz) French beans, halved

125g (4oz) shelled broad beans

50g (2oz) dried pastina (small soup pasta)

2 tbsp freshly chopped parsley

salt and freshly ground black pepper

pesto and freshly grated pecorino or
   Parmesan to serve

1 Heat the oil in a large pan. Add the onion, garlic, leek and rosemary and fry gently for 5–6 minutes or until softened but not coloured. Add the chickpeas with their liquid, the stock and tomatoes. Bring to the boil, then reduce the heat, cover the pan and simmer for 40 minutes.

2 Add the courgette, peas, French beans and broad beans. Bring back to the boil, then reduce the heat and simmer for 10 minutes. Add the pasta and parsley and simmer for 6–8 minutes until al dente. Season to taste with salt and ground black pepper.

3 Ladle into warmed bowls and serve topped with a spoonful of pesto and a sprinkling of cheese.

Serves 6

Special Soups

Perfect Soup Garnishes

Toasted Croûtons

1 Cut the crusts off sliced white bread, then cut into dice 1–2cm (½–¾in) square. Put the bread on a baking sheet and drizzle lightly with oil, then toss well with your hands.

2 Spread the bread dice in a single layer and bake at 200°C (180°C fan oven) mark 6 for 8–10 minutes until lightly browned.

Dairy

Cream and other dairy products such as yogurt and crème fraîche can also make a simple garnish, drizzled or spooned on to soup just before serving. They also add body and texture so use sparingly if the soup already includes cream.

Fried Croûtons

Croûtons fried in a generous amount of oil will crispen all over.

1. Cut the crusts off sliced white bread, then cut into dice 1–2cm (½–¾in) square.
2. Heat the oil medium-hot in a frying pan. Fry in a single layer, stirring constantly, until brown all over. Drain on kitchen paper.

Fresh herbs

A simple sprinkling of fresh herbs makes a delicious garnish for soups. Fresh herb flowers can also make a pretty and unusual garnish.

Chop the herbs just before serving, and choose a herb that complements that flavour of soup – for example, basil with tomato, chives with creamy soups, or coriander with Asian-style soups.

French Onion Soup

2 tbsp olive oil

6 large onions, about 1.6kg (3½lb), finely sliced

2 tsp fresh thyme leaves, plus extra to garnish

500ml (17fl oz) cider

1 tsp caster sugar

1.4 litres (2½ pints) vegetable stock (see page 13)

6 small slices white bread

150g (5oz) Gruyère, grated

salt and freshly ground black pepper

FREEZE AHEAD

To make ahead and freeze, prepare to the end of step 2 up to two months ahead. Cool completely, then empty into a freezerproof bag and freeze. To serve, thaw and complete the recipe to serve.

1 Gently heat the oil in a large pan. Add the onions, thyme and a large pinch of salt. Cover and cook over a low heat for 30 minutes, stirring occasionally, until the onions are soft.

2 Pour over the cider and add the sugar. Turn up the heat and bubble, stirring frequently, until the cider has evaporated and the onions are well caramelised, about 30–40 minutes.

3 Add the stock and heat through. Check the seasoning. Preheat the grill to medium. Put the bread on a baking tray and lightly toast both sides under the grill. Divide the cheese equally among the toasts and grill until melted and bubbling.

4 To serve, divide the soup among six warmed soup bowls. Top each bowl with a cheese toast and garnish with a few thyme leaves and ground black pepper.

Serves 6

Pea, Parmesan and Chorizo Soup

Hands-on time: 15 minutes
Cooking time: about 10 minutes

1 tbsp olive oil

1 large onion, roughly chopped

40g (1½oz) Parmesan, grated

75g (3oz) chorizo, skinned and finely cubed

750g (1lb 11oz) frozen peas

1.2 litre (2¼ pints) hot vegetable stock (see page 13)

salt and freshly ground black pepper

1 Preheat the oven to 220°C (200°C fan oven) mark 7. Heat the oil in a pan. Add the onion and fry for 5 minutes.

2 Meanwhile, sprinkle the Parmesan over a small non-stick baking sheet and cook in the oven for 5 minutes until golden and bubbling. Fry the chorizo in a small frying pan for 2–3 minutes until some of the oil has leaked out. Put to one side. Take the Parmesan out of the oven, leave to harden slightly, then use a spatula to lift the cheese off the baking sheet. Put on to a wire rack to cool.

3 Add the peas and hot stock to the onion pan and bring to the boil. Take off the heat and whiz the soup in a blender until smooth. Put back into the pan and check the seasoning.

4 To serve, reheat the soup if necessary, then divide among six warmed soup bowls. Break the Parmesan into shards. Garnish the soups with Parmesan shards, chorizo and chorizo oil. Serve immediately.

SAVE TIME

Make to the end of step 3 up to 2 hours ahead. Chill the soup and store the Parmesan and chorizo (in its pan) at room temperature. To serve, reheat the chorizo in the pan and complete the recipe to serve.

Serves 6

Broccoli and Basil Soup

Hands-on time: 25 minutes
Cooking time: 25 minutes

2 tbsp olive oil, plus extra to drizzle

1 large white onion, roughly chopped

1 large potato, peeled and roughly chopped

3 celery sticks, roughly chopped

1 head broccoli – about 375g (13oz), chopped

2 garlic cloves, peeled and chopped

1.3 litres (2¼ pints) vegetable stock (see page 13)

25g pack fresh basil

salt and freshly ground black pepper

crusty bread to serve

SAVE TIME

Make the soup to the end of step 3 up to 5 hours ahead. Transfer to a large bowl or jug. Leave to cool, then cover and chill. Cover the reserved basil with damp kitchen paper and chill. To serve, pour the soup back into a pan and reheat it over a medium heat until piping hot. Complete the recipe to serve.

1 Heat the oil in a large pan over a low-medium heat. Add the chopped onion, potato and celery and cook, stirring occasionally, for 5–10 minutes or until the vegetables are beginning to look translucent.

2 Add the broccoli, garlic and stock to the pan. Bring the mixture to the boil, then reduce the heat and simmer for 10 minutes – you need the vegetables to be just cooked through.

3 Add most of the basil and stalks to the soup saving a few pretty leaves to use as a garnish. Whiz the soup in a blender (in batches if necessary) until really smooth or use a stick blender to whiz it directly in the pan (off the heat). Pour the soup back into the empty pan and check the seasoning.

4 To serve, reheat the soup (if necessary), then ladle into six bowls. Drizzle over some oil, if you like, and garnish with the reserved basil leaves. Serve with crusty bread.

Serves 6

Watercress and Goat's Cheese Soup

Hands-on time: 25 minutes
Cooking time: 25 minutes

1 tbsp extra virgin olive oil, plus extra
  to drizzle

1 large onion, chopped

2 large garlic cloves, chopped

½ tsp freshly grated nutmeg

300g (11oz) watercress, plus extra to
  garnish (optional)

500g bag frozen spinach

1.6 litres (2¾ pints) hot vegetable stock
  (see page 13)

8 baguette slices, each 1.5cm (½in) thick

125g log goat's cheese

salt and freshly ground black pepper

1 Heat the oil in a large pan. Add the
  onion and gently cook for 15 minutes
  or until translucent and completely
  soft. Stir in the garlic, nutmeg and lots
  of seasoning and cook for 1 minute.

2 Add the watercress and frozen
  spinach, then add the hot stock.

Bring to the boil. Whiz the soup in a
blender (in batches if necessary) until
completely smooth then pour it back
into the pan and check the seasoning,
adding more nutmeg, if you like.

3 Preheat the grill to medium. Arrange
  the baguette slices on a baking tray
  and toast on one side until golden.
  Meanwhile, cut the goat's cheese log
  into eight equal round slices. Turn
  the baguette slices, then lay a piece of
  goat's cheese on each. Put back under
  the grill and cook until the cheese is
  golden and melting.

4 Reheat the soup and ladle into eight
  warmed soup bowls. Drizzle over
  some extra virgin olive oil, sprinkle
  over some black pepper and float a
  goat's cheese toast in each bowl (or
  serve separately). Garnish with extra
  watercress, if you like, and serve
  immediately.

Serves 8

Bloody Mary Soup

Hands-on time: 25 minutes
Cooking time: about 45 minutes

1 red onion, roughly chopped

3 garlic cloves, crushed

2 celery sticks, roughly chopped, plus
    extra sticks to garnish

600g (1lb 5oz) ripe tomatoes, halved
    (the redder the better!)

1 red chilli, seeded and roughly chopped
    (see page 78)

2 tbsp olive oil

½ tsp celery salt – use plain salt if
    you prefer

600ml (1 pint) vegetable stock
    (see page 13)

400g can chopped tomatoes

3 tbsp tomato purée

1 tbsp Worcestershire sauce

salt and freshly ground black pepper

crème fraîche or double cream and
    vodka to serve

1 Preheat the oven to 200°C (180°C fan oven) mark 6. Put the onion, garlic, celery, fresh tomatoes, chilli, oil, celery salt and plenty of pepper into a large roasting tin. Toss together and roast for 40 minutes.

2 Scrape the roasted vegetable mixture into a blender and whiz until completely smooth. Strain through a fine sieve into a large pan (work the pulp hard to extract as much flavour as possible). Discard any skins and seeds that won't go through the sieve.

3 Add the stock to the pan, then the canned tomatoes, tomato purée and Worcestershire sauce. Stir to combine and check the seasoning.

4 To serve, reheat the soup gently. Ladle into six sturdy glasses or large coffee cups. Add a celery stick to each glass/cup and garnish with a dollop of crème fraîche or a swirl of cream. Serve small shots of vodka alongside, which people can stir into their soup if they like.

Serves 6

Roasted Garlic and Almond Soup

Hands-on time: 25 minutes
Cooking time: 45 minutes

1–2 bulbs of garlic, depending on
    preferred strength, unpeeled

1 shallot, peeled and halved

2 tbsp olive oil, plus extra to drizzle

200g (7oz) flaked almonds

250g (9oz) bloomer loaf, cut into
    2.5cm (1in) chunks

200ml (7fl oz) whole milk

1 litre (1¾ pints) vegetable stock
    (see page 13)

pinch of sugar (optional)

salt and freshly ground black pepper

1 tbsp finely chopped fresh chives
    to garnish

1 Preheat the oven to 220°C (200°C fan
oven) mark 7. Roughly break up the
garlic bulbs. Wrap the garlic cloves,
shallot halves, 1 tbsp of the oil and
some seasoning in a double layer
of foil and cook in the oven for 20
minutes. Open the parcel and cook
for a further 15–20 minutes until the
garlic and shallots are tender and
lightly golden.

2 Meanwhile, scatter the almonds on
a baking tray and put into the oven.
Cook for a few minutes until lightly
golden. Tip into a bowl and put to one
side. Next, scatter 150g (5oz) of the
bread chunks on the baking tray and
toss through the remaining oil and
some seasoning. Cook in the oven for
8–10 minutes until golden, then put to
one side.

3 Keep a handful of the toasted almonds
for the garnish to one side, then put
the rest in a large pan with the milk,
stock and remaining uncooked bread
chunks. Add the cooked shallot, then
squeeze in the softened garlic from
inside each clove and discard the
skins (snip off the root with scissors
and squeeze out paste). Heat gently
until the bread has dissolved, then
whiz the soup in a blender (in batches
if necessary) until smooth.

4 Pour the soup back into the pan and reheat gently. Season to taste with salt, ground black pepper and a pinch of sugar, if needed. Ladle into shallow bowls, drizzle over a little oil and sprinkle with chives and the reserved almonds. Serve with the croûtons.

Serves 6

Black Olive Bread

To make 2 loaves, you will need: 2 tsp traditional dried yeast, 500g (1lb 2oz) strong white bread flour, plus extra to dust, 2 tsp coarse salt, plus extra to sprinkle, 6 tbsp extra virgin olive oil, plus extra to grease, 100g (3½oz) black olives, pitted and chopped.

1 Put 150ml (¼ pint) hand-hot water into a jug, stir in the yeast and leave for 10 minutes or until foamy. Put the flour into a bowl or a food processor, then add the salt, yeast mix, 200ml (7fl oz) warm water and 2 tbsp oil. Mix using a wooden spoon or the dough hook for 2-3 minutes to make a soft smooth dough. Put the dough in a lightly oiled bowl; cover with oiled clingfilm and leave in a warm place for 45 minutes or until doubled in size.

2 Punch the dough to knock out the air, then knead on a lightly floured worksurface for 1 minute. Add the olives and knead until combined. Divide in half, shape into rectangles and put into two greased tins, each about 25.5 × 15cm (10 × 6in). Cover with clingfilm and leave in a warm place for 1 hour or until the dough is puffy.

3 Preheat the oven to 200°C (180°C fan oven) mark 6. Press your finger into the dough 12 times, drizzle over 2 tbsp oil and sprinkle with salt. Bake for 30-35 minutes until golden. Drizzle with the remaining oil. Slice and serve warm.

Griddled Garlic Bread

To serve eight, you will need: 175g
(6oz) butter, cubed, 3 garlic cloves,
crushed, 1 bunch of stiff-stemmed
fresh thyme sprigs, 1 large crusty loaf,
cut into 2cm (¾in) thick slices, salt
and freshly ground black pepper.

1 Preheat a griddle pan. Put the
   butter and garlic into a pan over
   a gentle heat and leave to melt.
   Season with salt and pepper.
2 Dip the thyme into the melted
   butter and brush one side of each
   slice of bread. Put the slices,
   buttered side down, in the griddle
   pan and cook for 1–2 minutes
   until crisp and golden. Brush
   the uppermost sides with the
   remaining butter, turn
   over and cook the other side.
   Serve immediately.

Butternut Squash Soup with Cheesy Toasts

Hands-on time: 30 minutes
Cooking time: 35 minutes

For the soup

2 tbsp extra virgin olive oil, plus extra
to drizzle

5 fresh sage leaves

1 large onion, finely chopped

2 celery sticks, finely chopped

2 medium carrots, finely chopped

1 butternut squash, about 900g (2lb),
peeled, seeded and cut into rough
2.5cm (1in pieces)

1.3 litres (2¼ pints) vegetable stock
(see page 13)

salt and freshly ground black pepper

For the cheesy toasts

6 slices bread

100g (3½oz) Cheddar or Parmesan,
grated

few pinches dried chilli flakes

few dashes Worcestershire sauce
(optional)

1 Heat the oil in a large pan and add the
sage leaves. Cook for 30 seconds or
until crisp. Lift out the leaves with a
slotted spoon (leaving any oil behind)
and put on kitchen paper (the leaves
will be used as a garnish).

2 To the pan, add the onion, celery,
carrots and squash. Cook for
10 minutes, stirring occasionally,
until the vegetables are beginning
to soften. Pour in the stock and bring
to the boil, then reduce the heat and
simmer gently for 20 minutes or until
the vegetables are completely soft.

3 Whiz the soup in a blender (in batches
if necessary) until smooth, then
pour back into the pan. Check the
seasoning and put to one side.

4 To make the cheesy toasts, preheat the
grill to medium. Lay the bread slices
out on a baking tray, then grill on both
sides until toasted and lightly golden.
Divide the cheese, chilli flakes and

Worcestershire sauce, if using, among the toasts and grill until golden and bubbling. Reheat the soup if necessary and ladle into six warmed soup bowls. Garnish with a drizzle of oil and the crumbled fried sage leaves. Serve with the cheesy toasts.

Serves 6

Spectacular Swirled Soup

Hands-on time: 15 minutes
Cooking time: 1 hour

600g (1lb 5oz) fresh beetroot, unpeeled
but trimmed

1 large onion, unpeeled and halved

2 celery sticks

3 garlic cloves, unpeeled

1.1 litre (2 pints) chicken stock
(see page 14)

400g (14oz) fresh peas

salt and freshly ground black pepper

a small handful of fresh curly parsley,
roughly chopped, to garnish

1 Preheat the oven to 200°C (180°C fan oven) mark 6. Wrap each beetroot and onion half separately in foil. Next, wrap the celery sticks together in foil and finally the garlic. Put the parcels in a roasting tin and cook for 1 hour or until tender.

2 Unwrap the vegetables when cool enough to handle. Peel the beetroot and onion. Roughly chop the beetroot and put into a blender with half the onion, 1 roasted celery stick and 600ml (a little over 1 pint) stock.

Squeeze the roasted garlic from two of the cloves, discarding the skins, and add to the mixture. Blend until smooth. Empty the soup into a pan and check the seasoning.

3 Meanwhile, bring a pan of water to the boil. Cook the peas for 2 minutes or until tender. Drain.

4 Rinse the blender. Add the cooked peas, plus the remaining onion, celery and stock. Squeeze out the remaining roasted garlic, discarding the skin, and add to the pea mixture. Blend until smooth. Empty the soup into a separate pan and check the seasoning.

5 Gently reheat both soups, then pour each into a separate jug. With one jug in each hand, pour the soups at the same time into a bowl. Crack over some black pepper and swirl the soups quickly with a skewer. Repeat with the remaining bowls, then garnish with parsley and serve immediately.

Make the soups up to a day in advance. After blending, empty into two bowls. Cool, then cover and chill. Reheat in separate pans and complete the recipe to serve.

Serves 8

Golden Lentil and Chorizo Soup

Hands-on time: 15 minutes
Cooking time: about 30 minutes

50g (2oz) chorizo, cubed

1 large leek, finely sliced

2 celery sticks, chopped

2 carrots, finely chopped

125g (4oz) red lentils, washed

1.3 litres (2¼ pints) vegetable stock
  (see page 13)

salt and freshly ground black pepper

1 tbsp pumpkin seeds to garnish

1 Heat a large pan and fry the chorizo for 2 minutes, until it gives up some of its oil. Empty the chorizo and oil into a small bowl and put to one side.

2 Put the pan back on to the heat and add the leek, celery and carrots. Cook gently for 10 minutes or until the vegetables are softening. Add the lentils and stock and bring to the boil. Reduce the heat and simmer for 20 minutes or until the lentils are soft.

3 Whiz the soup in a blender until smooth (in batches if necessary) and pour back into the pan to reheat, if necessary. Check the seasoning. Serve in warmed soup bowls, topped with the chorizo, a drizzle of chorizo oil and the pumpkin seeds.

Serves 4

278 cal ♥ 13g protein
5g fat (1g sat) ♥ 13g fibre
46g carb ♥ 1.7g salt

10

140 cal ♥ 1g protein
11g fat (7g sat) ♥ 2g fibre
10g carb ♥ 0.2g salt

16

117 cal ♥ 3g protein
6g fat (4g sat) ♥ 4g fibre
13g carb ♥ 0.1g salt

18

158 cal ♥ 4g protein
12g fat (2g sat) ♥ 3g fibre
10g carb ♥ 0.2g salt

20

Calorie Gallery

323 cal ♥ 30g protein
14g fat (5g sat) ♥ 13g fibre
19g carb ♥ 3g salt

30

265 cal ♥ 37g protein
10g fat (2g sat) ♥ 3g fibre
5g carb ♥ 0.4g salt

34

106 cal ♥ 6g protein
7g fat (1g sat) ♥ 2.3g fibre
5g carb ♥ trace salt

40

without vegetable crisps
113 cal ♥ 3g protein
5g fat (2g sat) ♥ 3g fibre
14g carb ♥ 0.6g salt

52

143 cal ♥ 7g protein
5g fat (0.7g sat) ♥ 6g fibre
19g carb ♥ 0.8g salt

54

143 cal ♥ 3g protein
12g fat (7g sat) ♥ 1.6g fibre
6g carb ♥ 0.9g salt

56

185 cal ♥ 3g protein
12g fat (7g sat) ♥ 4g fibre
16g carb ♥ 0.7g salt

72

188 cal ♥ 7g protein
10g fat (4g sat) ♥ 6g fibre
17g carb ♥ 0.1g salt

74

248 cal ♥ 22g protein
10g fat (2g sat) ♥ 2g fibre
12g carb ♥ 0.8g salt

76

241 cal ♥ 30g protein
16g fat (1g sat) ♥ 2g fibre
18g carb ♥ 1.1g salt

80

219 cal ♥ 11g protein
16g fat (9g sat) ♥ 5g fibre
7g carb ♥ 1.3g salt

22

139 cal ♥ 14g protein
3g fat (2g sat) ♥ 0.7g fibre
13g carb ♥ 0.9g salt

24

338 cal ♥ 38g protein
10g fat (3g sat) ♥ 3g fibre
27g carb ♥ 1.8g salt

26

432 cal ♥ 20g protein
20g fat (7g sat) ♥ 5g fibre
46g carb ♥ 1.8g salt

28

321 cal ♥ 5g protein
22g fat (5g sat) ♥ 6g fibre
25g carb ♥ 1.1g salt

42

70 cal ♥ 2g protein
1.5g fat (0.3g sat) ♥ 1.4g fibre
11g carb ♥ 0.4g salt

44

109 cal ♥ 2g protein
2g fat (0.3g sat) ♥ 2.2g fibre
20g carb ♥ 0.8g salt

48

80 cal ♥ 3g protein
1.2g fat (0.1g sat) ♥ 7g fibre
14g carb ♥ 0.8g salt

50

342 cal ♥ 8g protein
21.4g fat (1.6g sat) ♥ 2.5g fibre
29g carb ♥ 0.9g salt

58

128 cal ♥ 3g protein
9.5g fat (5.6g sat) ♥ 3g fibre
8g carb ♥ 0.8g salt

60

312 cal ♥ 17g protein
8g fat (1g sat) ♥ 18g fibre
44g carb ♥ 3g salt

68

346 cal ♥ 5g protein
26g fat (20g sat) ♥ 3g fibre
24g carb ♥ 0.6g salt

70

284 cal ♥ 43g protein
3g fat (1g sat) ♥ 3g fibre
22g carb ♥ 1.7g salt

82

431 cal ♥ 32g protein
25g fat (7g sat) ♥ 2g fibre
20g carb ♥ 1.5g salt

84

215 cal ♥ 15g protein
13g fat (3g sat) ♥ 1g fibre
11g carb ♥ 1.2g salt

86

343 cal ♥ 33g protein
14g fat (7g sat) ♥ 4g fibre
22g carb ♥ 0.8g salt

88

517 cal ♥ 34g protein
21g fat (8g sat) ♥ 6g fibre
51g carb ♥ 0.8g salt

90

with 1 slice of cornbread
359 cal ♥ 25g protein
4g fat (1g sat) ♥ 6g fibre
64g carb ♥ 0.5g salt

94

121 cal ♥ 5g protein
6g fat (1g sat) ♥ 2g fibre
11g carb ♥ 0.9g salt

96

107 cal ♥ 6g protein
4g fat (trace sat) ♥ 2g fibre
9g carb ♥ 1g salt

98

Calorie Gallery

370 cal ♥ 35g protein
8g fat (2g sat) ♥ 3g fibre
41g carb ♥ 1.2g salt

112

274 cal ♥ 20g protein
9g fat (3g sat) ♥ 2g fibre
31g carb ♥ 2.0g salt

114

538 cal ♥ 45g protein
34g fat (19g sat) ♥ 3g fibre
13g carb ♥ 2.1g salt

122

371 cal ♥ 34g protein
15g fat (6g sat) ♥ 6g fibre
25g carb ♥ 2.7g salt

134

526cal ♥ 33g protein
29g fat (16g sat) ♥ 4g fibre
34g carb ♥ 4.7g salt

136

302 cal ♥ 26g protein
6g fat (4g sat) ♥ 4g fibre
37g carb ♥ 0.4g salt

138

180 cal ♥ 13g protein
9g fat (3g sat) ♥ 7g fibre
14g carb ♥ 1.3g salt

152

95 cal ♥ 4g protein
5g fat (1g sat) ♥ 3g fibre
9g carb ♥ 0.5g salt

154

152 cal ♥ 9g protein
7g fat (3g sat) ♥ 3g fibre
15g carb ♥ 1.3g salt

156

83 cal ♥ 2g protein
4g fat (1g sat) ♥ 3g fibre
9g carb ♥ 0.7g salt

158

239 cal ♥ 3g protein
16g fat (6g sat) ♥ 4g fibre
15g carb ♥ 0.4g salt

02

157 cal ♥ 6g protein
4g fat (1g sat) ♥ 4g fibre
25g carb ♥ 1.2g salt

104

130 cal ♥ 7g protein
4g fat (1g sat) ♥ 1g fibre
18g carb ♥ 1g salt

108

123 cal ♥ 4g protein
10g fat (5g sat) ♥ 2g fibre
6g carb ♥ 0.8g salt

110

278 cal ♥ 25g protein
12g fat (3g sat) ♥ 3g fibre
18g carb ♥ 1.2g salt

24

354 cal ♥ 21g protein
19g fat (7g sat) ♥ 7g fibre
25g carb ♥ 0.2g salt

126

257 cal ♥ 5g protein
9g fat (4.5g sat) ♥ 9g fibre
39g carb ♥ 0.9g salt

128

231 cal ♥ 14g protein
5g fat (2g sat) ♥ 5g fibre
33g carb ♥ 1g salt

130

184 cal ♥ 4g protein
8g fat (1g sat) ♥ 4g fibre
21g carb ♥ 1.3g salt

40

184 cal ♥ 11g protein
3g fat (0.5g sat) ♥ 6g fibre
28g carb ♥ 0.6g salt

142

195 cal ♥ 9g protein
8.2g fat (1.2g sat) ♥ 9g fibre
22g carb ♥ 0.8g salt

144

336 cal ♥ 13g protein
14g fat (6g sat) ♥ 4g fibre
35g carb ♥ 1.3g salt

150

371 cal ♥ 14g protein
25g fat (3g sat) ♥ 0.8g fibre
25g carb ♥ 1.1g salt

60

250 cal ♥ 19g protein
11g fat (4g sat) ♥ 5g fibre
32g carb ♥ 1.3g salt

164

75 cal ♥ 5g protein
1g fat (0g sat) ♥ 6g fibre
12g carb ♥ 0.5g salt

166

178 cal ♥ 12g protein
5g fat (2g sat) ♥ 5g fibre
23g carb ♥ 1g salt

168

Index

PICTURE CREDITS
Photographers:
Neil Barclay (page 127); Steve
Baxter (page 29); Nicki Dowey
(pages 17, 21, 23, 25, 41, 43, 45, 51,
53, 57, 59, 61, 69, 71, 73, 75, 77, 81, 85,
87, 89, 99, 109, 129, 131, 141, 143 and
145); Fiona Kennedy (page 139);
Gareth Morgans (pages 27, 31, 91,
105, 115, 123, 135 and 169); Myles
New (pages 113, 151 and 157); Craig
Robertson (pages 8, 12, 15, 19, 32,
33, 35, 46, 47, 49, 55, 78, 79, 100,
101, 103, 106, 107, 132, 133, 137, 148,
149 and 163); Maja Smend (pages
155 and 165); Sam Stowell (pages
159 and 161); Lucinda Symons
(page 111); Philip Webb (page 97);
Jon Whitaker (pages 95 and 125);
Kate Whitaker (pages 11, 83, 153
and 167).

Home Economists:
Joanna Farrow, Emma Jane Frost,
Teresa Goldfinch, Alice Hart Lucy
McKelvie, Kim Morphew, Aya
Nishimura, Bridget Sargeson, Kate
Trend and Mari Mererid Williams.

Stylists:
Tamzin Ferdinando, Wei Tang,
Helen Trent and Fanny Ward.

BAKE ME A CAKE
There's always time for cake

EASY PEASY MEALS
Easy meals for every day

LET'S DO BRUNCH
Mouth-watering meals to start your day

CHEAP EATS
Budget-busting ideas that won't break the bank

WONDERFUL ONE-POTS
Easy peasy recipes made in just one pot

Available online at store.anovabooks.com and from all good bookshops

SUPER SOUPS
Sumptuous soups for every day

SKINNY SUPPERS
Delicious, nutritious recipes under 300 calories

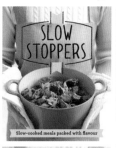
SLOW STOPPERS
Slow-cooked meals packed with flavour

GREAT VEG
Inspired ideas for delicious veggie meals

AL FRESCO EATS
Easy grills, barbecues and picnics

ROAST IT
There's nothing better than a delicious roast

FLASH IN THE PAN
Spice up your noodles and stir-fries

GLUTEN-FREE AND EASY
Oh-so-good-for-you recipes that taste great

LOW FAT LOW CAL
Nice recipes don't need to be naughty